Garden Plants

For Free

TONY DERRICK

A QUINTET BOOK
produced for
GALLERY BOOKS
An imprint of W.H. Smith Publishers Inc.
112 Madison Avenue
New York, New York 10016

ISBN 0-8317-3762-X

This book was designed and produced by
Quintet Publishing Limited
6 Blundell Street
London N7 9BH

Creative Director: Peter Bridgewater
Designer: Stuart Walden
Editor: Shaun Barrington

Typeset in Great Britain by
Central Southern Typesetters, Eastbourne
Manufactured in Hong Kong by
Regent Publishing Services Limited
Printed in Hong Kong by
Leefung-Asco Printers Limited

Contents

INTRODUCTION
AND BASIC
TECHNIQUES

Introduction

There is a special excitement in creating new plants, from seeds or from parts of an existing plant. It brings a sense of achievement and of developing skill. With a little know-how, which you can acquire from this book, and some close care, you can turn one mature plant into a generous group in a border, or enough for several in different parts of your garden.

Propagating your own plants obviously saves you the expense of buying many plants – an undeniable advantage; but for most gardeners it is the feeling of pride after successful propagation that is the real reward.

If you find propagating fascinates you, why not make a hobby of it? Give any surplus plants to friends or offer them for sale for a charity – or if you prefer, sell them to a nurseryman, to defray your running costs. And once you have mastered the simple methods described here, do try your hand at more challenging things like budding and grafting.

Enjoy a rich tapestry of flowers and foliage at little cost by raising your own from seeds and cuttings.

Basic Methods of Propagation

Garden plants are propagated in a variety of ways. Some respond to several different methods, others to only one. It is part of the gardener's skill to select the most suitable method for his plant and particular circumstances.

All the methods described here are comparatively simple, but they still need to be carried out carefully and accurately to ensure satisfying results. So, though you will probably be eager to turn straight to the methods themselves, do study all the other introductory sections, so that you can provide your cuttings and seedlings with the right conditions and aftercare and defend them from insect and fungal enemies.

SEEDS

Raising seed is the first method to spring to mind, since it is nature's own. Many kinds of seeds will readily germinate at the right time of year in the open ground, but others will need to be sown in pots or trays in a greenhouse or cold frame or on a light windowsill and gradually accustomed to outdoor conditions when they are large enough.

To get plants absolutely for free, you will want to save and sow seeds from your own plants. But be warned. While seeds from species – kinds that occur in nature – will produce progeny nearly identical to their parents, choice garden hybrids and special selections are more likely to give you inferior results as they revert to some earlier type in the plant's heredity. To succeed with such plants you will need to propagate them from a stem or root or division, which will faithfully reproduce their special characteristics, or go back to the seedsman for professionally raised seeds.

When you do save seeds from your own plants, make sure they are ripe, or nearly so. Collect them before the pods or capsules burst and the seeds are dispersed, if necessary tying bags over them to catch any seeds that fall. Seeds that are not fully ripe when autumn days turn damp, cold and misty will have to be taken under cover and ripened in the warm. Cut the whole seedhead, put it safely in an envelope, then spread on a plate in a cool greenhouse or on a sunny windowsill until ready. Sift or shake until the seeds can be packeted or put in airtight tins until sowing time comes round.

Some seeds, though ripe, will not germinate until their dormancy has been broken. Berberis and holly, for instance, must be stratified – that is, the seeds are spread between layers of sharp sand in a pan and left outdoors at the foot of a cold wall to be frosted. (Protect them from mice and other vermin with small mesh wire netting, or they could be eaten.) By spring they should be ready for sowing like other seeds.

Seed Sowing Indoors

Assemble suitable compost, clean pots or trays, seeds and labels to identify them before you start.

When sown, seeds should not be so close together that seedlings will be overcrowded when they germinate.

SEED-SOWING OUTDOORS

To succeed, choose a reasonably fertile patch of ground in good light and prepare it by forking it over, removing any weeds or other obstructions and break down any lumps. Tread it fairly firm, but not hard, then rake the surface down to a fine crumbly consistency. Water and leave to soak in if the soil is very dry.

Draw shallow drills (furrows) in the surface, about ½in (12mm) deep, then sow seeds thinly along the drill. Rake soil gently back to refill the drill and firm lightly in place with the head of the rake, so the seeds are in close contact with the soil. Mark ends of rows with canes and label with the name of the plant.

Loosely fill the container with compost, rap its base on the bench to settle and level it, then lightly firm surface to leave 6cm (¼in) below rim.

Tip some seeds into the palm of your hand, then sow thinly over compost surface – or sow direct from a corner of the packet.

Scatter a very shallow layer of compost over the seeds to cover them and keep them moist until they grow.

Water in gently with a fine-rose can or hand sprayer. Cover with a pane of glass or plastic. Ventilate daily. Keep warm.

When the seedlings are large enough, lift them carefully with a hand-fork and set out separately at a suitable spacing in nursery rows to grow larger without overcrowding. Plant out in their permanent positions later in the season when large enough to fend for themselves.

SEED-SOWING INDOORS

The principles are the same, but the scale is smaller and the conditions artificially controlled. Fill pots or trays with an open-textured mix specially formulated for seed-sowing, firm lightly in place, level surface and water and allow to drain.

Again, sow the seeds thinly to avoid later overcrowding and cover with a shallow layer of the same compost. Cover the container with a sheet of glass or clear plastic and some paper to keep in moisture; shade it from bright light until seedlings appear, then promptly remove coverings, but make sure seedlings cannot get scorched.

As soon as the seedlings are large enough to handle, lift them carefully with a label, so their roots are not damaged and transplant them into trays of soil-mixture to give them more space. Handle them by their leaves, not by their vulnerable stems and set them gently at the right depth in small holes made in the soil with a wooden dibber. Push soil around them and firm lightly with your fingers. Water, ventilate, shade and feed as necessary so they grow into strong young plants ready for transplanting into pots or outdoors.

Hardwood cuttings are taken in autumn and rooted outdoors in slits in the ground with sharp sand in the base.

Softwood cuttings are taken in spring and need close warm conditions to root.

CUTTINGS

Stem cuttings provide a convenient means of propagating many kinds of plant, so the youngsters match their parents exactly. They fall into three categories according to the ripeness or woodiness of their stems. Each is taken at a different time of year and treated in its own way. *Softwood* cuttings are generally about 2in (5cm) long and taken in early summer and need close, warm (about 65°–70°F, 18°–21°C), humid greenhouse (or windowsill) conditions to root. They can be taken from young sideshoots of shrubs or as basal shoots arising from lupins, dahlias or delphiniums.

Semi-hardwood cuttings, of which bedding geranium (pelargonium) cuttings are typical, are 3–4in (7.5–10cm) long, firmer and rooted in pots but without specially warm or close conditions. *Hardwood* cuttings, 10–14in (25–35cm) long, generally of shrubs and woody plants, are taken in

Half ripe cuttings, like those of bedding geraniums, are rooted in pots but need only moderate warmth and minimum attention.

Air layering a rhododendron

mid-autumn and inserted and overwintered in the open ground. Most root by the spring.

Whatever the type of cutting, select healthy shoots of typical growth with strong stems – neither flabby nor thin and weak. Trim across just beneath a leaf joint, where new roots most readily develop, remove all the lower leaves, so they are not buried where they will rot. Dip in hormone rooting compound, powder or liquid, then insert in a suitable rooting mixture. This is generally gritty with an open texture but low in plant foods. When the cuttings have rooted strongly they should then be moved into a more nourishing mixture which includes soil and probably fertilizers too.

Leaf bud cuttings are related kinds of cuttings in which a piece of stem bearing just one leaf bud is prepared and rooted in warmth. Leaf bud cuttings of camellias are taken in late summer and inserted upright in the rooting compost. Grapevines are propagated from single bud cuttings with about an inch of hardwood stem either side of the bud. These are usually inserted horizontally in the surface of the soil mix after removing a sliver of wood from the lower side, and rooted at about 70°F (21°C).

LAYERING

This is a method of propagating that consists of rooting shoots while they are still attached to the parent plant and drawing nourishment from it. It occurs naturally on some shrubs, such as *Jasminum nudiflorum,* the winter jasmine,

and *Forsythia suspensa.* If one of their drooping shoots touches the soil, it is likely to develop roots, anchor itself there and start drawing nutriment from a fresh patch of ground. It is then simple for the gardener to sever the daughter plant from its parent, lift it carefully, so its roots are not damaged, and plant it (or pot it) where it is required to flower. Truly plants for free!

To imitate nature's behaviour, select a low-growing shoot that can be bent down to the soil, wound it where you want it to root by cutting it diagonally about half way through and prop the wound open with a sliver of wood. You could treat the wound with a hormone rooting preparation to make doubly sure of success. Peg down the shoot with a doubled-over wire pin, cover it with soil – or better still a sand/peat potting mixture that will encourage rooting – and stake the tip of the shoot upright so it will form a shapely plant when rooted and severed from its parent.

If layered in spring, a shoot should be rooted well enough to be cut from its parent in autumn and transplanted to a nursery bed to continue developing before it is eventually planted in its permanent position.

Tip layering is a related phenomenon, often seen on blackberry canes, for example. A long pendulous cane will form strong roots at its tip if it touches the soil and develop a new plant there. This could, of course, be severed and transplanted where required and will reproduce its parents' characteristics exactly.

Dividing perennials

Cut down the top growth

Lift with a fork

Divide up, pulling apart with the hands or levering with a fork

Plant out small vigorous pieces in prepared ground

LEFT: A modern garden

AIR LAYERING

This is an ingenious development of layering in which the gardener brings the soil to the branch instead of bending it down to the soil. In this way we can layer many shrubs and trees that are not pliant enough to reach the ground.

A suitable shoot is cut upwards through the centre for 2–3in (5–7.5cm) and the wound held open with a matchstick while it is treated with rooting hormone, then filled and surrounded by moist sphagnum moss, when the matchstick is removed. The shoot and moss are then enclosed in a bandage of clear plastic film to keep in moisture while roots form. When the roots become visible, the shoot can then be severed from its parent plant and potted up. Keep it warm and close for a while until it becomes established, then gradually introduce it to normal conditions.

Runners, as formed by strawberry plants, are similar in principle to tip layers, since a plant forms at the end of each runner sent out by the plant. But it subsequently extends beyond the plant to form more young plants. When using this technique to propagate strawberries, a gardener will take only one plantlet – the first and strongest – from each runner. It is usual to root the plantlets straight into pots of potting compost so that, when severed from the parent, they can be planted out with the minimum of root disturbance and establish quickly.

DIVISION

This is one of the most commonly used methods, particularly among clump-forming border plants, as it is so simple and effective. Just lift vigorous well-established clumps and divide them by pulling them apart with your hands, levering them apart with two hand-forks or border forks back to back, or resort to a knife. Select young healthy pieces with some good roots from the outside of the clump to provide new plants.

Division is normally undertaken in autumn or early spring. The hardest kinds like asters (Michaelmas daisies) can be divided in autumn or early winter, as their divisions are sure to survive the rigours of winter. But more tender kinds like pyrethrums are best left until early spring or even until just after they have flowered to avoid losses during winter following the shock of being torn apart.

It is inadvisable to divide plants in full leaf or flower, as the shock will result in at least temporary collapse. But if this is your only opportunity to secure stock of some desirable plant, you might risk it. Be prepared to lose the top growth for that season and to have to nurse the plant for some weeks until its roots have had a chance to re-establish. With care, you should have plants able to face the winter and give you a worthwhile display the next summer.

Root cuttings

Provide sharp drainage when propagating from root cuttings.

Lifted clump of *Phlox decussata,* showing thicker roots used as cuttings.

Lay 8cm (3in) lengths of root on surface of rooting compost, then lightly cover.

OFFSETS

Some plants, like *Sedum spathulifolium* and various sempervivums are typical offset formers, spreading clumps of leaf rosettes. Each of these rosettes may be removed with a short stem and a few roots and inserted in a gritty compost, where they will soon form independent plants. With little more attention than this, rosettes *without* roots can be encouraged to root and form new plants. In fact, you may find rosettes disturbed by foraging birds rooting into promising soil around a plant in the garden. Once you have one of these rosette-forming plants, you need never be without plenty of replacements and gifts for friends.

ROOT CUTTINGS

A number of border plants will obligingly make new plants from pieces of their thick fleshy roots. You may discover this by accident as I did by transplanting an acanthus and leaving some of its roots behind. It soon developed into an extra plant.

To propagate in this way, just scrape soil away from one side of a clump of the plant and cut away suitable lengths of root, about 1½in (2.8cm) long. Trim them straight across the top, slanting at the base, to make sure you get them the right way up, then insert into a gritty mixture suitable for cuttings, their tops level with the surface, to grow – usually without extra heat.

Phlox decussata is the typical example of a variant of this method. Take short lengths of its ⅛in (3mm) thick roots and lay them flat on the surface of a similar soil mixture, covering with a thin layer. These cuttings will also make new plants – and incidentally avoid transmitting any stem eelworm that may be in your phlox plants. Mint (culinary and ornamental) roots in the same way.

LILY SCALES AND BULBILS

Healthy lily bulbs, formed of loose fleshy scales, offer you an easy way of making more plants. Detach one or two scales from each bulb – do not take too many unless you are desperate to make a lot, or you will weaken the parent – and put them in a clear plastic bag of moist peat and sand mixture in a warm place. Each will develop a tiny plant at the base of the scale, and they can be set out in trays of soil-less or peat-based mix to grow on.

A few lilies, of which *Lilium tigrinum* and the popular variety 'Enchantment' are most widely grown, form bulbils up their stems. These, about the size of sugar peas, can be detached when fully developed in midsummer and sown like seeds in trays to form more young lily plants – a real gift for the gardener!

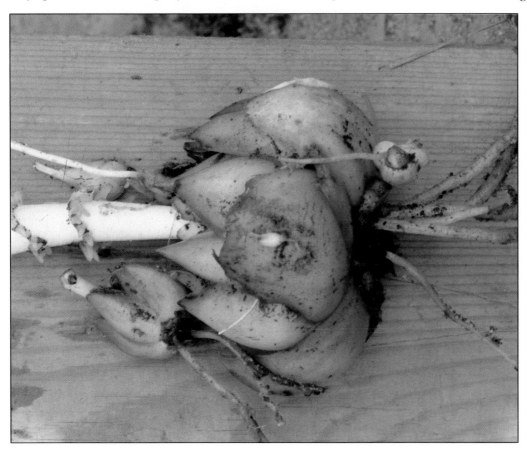

Bulb of *Lilium speciosum,*
showing plump scales used to
form new young bulbs.

When to Propagate

The most suitable time to propagate the plants in this book varies widely according to the type of plant and the method used. Spring is the most favoured time, since there is then a burst of vigour after the winter dormancy and a long growing season lies ahead during which the new plant can become well established before it has to face the rigours of its first winter.

But while many seeds and cuttings are started in early or mid spring for these reasons, perennials and biennials tend to be sown in late spring, so that they are not too advanced by the onset of winter, but form sturdy, compact plants to pass safely through the severest weather.

Softwood, semi-hardwood and hardwood stem cuttings are taken at different times (as explained under *Cuttings*) according to their development and in order to get the cuttings established in time to stand either the winter or summer, as the case may be.

Root cuttings can be taken in late winter and are little trouble. Strawberries are rooted from runners in mid-summer, then planted out in late summer. Offsets of sedums and sempervivums can be taken at almost any time, though reasonable warmth helps them root.

Finally, bear in mind that the right time to propagate some plants is *never* – that is, if they are infected with some dreaded viral disease, for instance, in which case they should be destroyed. Other plants may be troubled by greenfly, red spider mites or mildew. You must then get them safely cleaned up before thinking of making more of them, or you will spread the trouble with the plant.

OPPOSITE TOP Basic tools for indoor propagating – plastic pots, watering can, sprayer, canes and maximum-minimum thermometer.

OPPOSITE BELOW Invest in best-quality cutting tools that stay sharp – secateurs, pruning and budding knives, plus stout gloves to protect your hands.

Equipment

As the title of this book implies, you do not need to spend a great deal of money on tools and equipment to succeed at simple propagating. But such equipment as you do buy should be of good quality and right for the job.

Tools for taking and preparing cuttings should have really sharp stainless steel blades. Buy a budding knife, an efficient two-bladed pair of secateurs with scissors action (as the anvil type tends to crush and injure soft stems, which can then rot) and possibly a scalpel for the cleanest cuts, from a reputable garden centre or nursery.

You will need a range of pots and seed trays for germinating seeds and rooting cuttings. The most useful pot sizes are 2½in (6cm), 3½in (9cm), 4½in (11cm) and 5in (13cm), plus some shallower 5½in (14cm) half-pots and standard-sized seed trays. How many of each you buy will depend on how much propagating you are undertaking and what types.

You will need a choice of soil-based and peat-based seed and potting mixtures, plus some sharp sand, perlite or vermiculite to add to their porosity, and peat to improve their texture and moisture retention. A mixture of peat and sand or perlite will be fine for rooting many cuttings.

To ensure efficient rooting of cuttings, you should get some rooting hormone, powder or liquid. Even where it is not essential, it gives one added confidence.

To insert cuttings or seedlings into their growing medium without damaging them, make a small wooden dibber from a piece of dowel ⅜in (1cm) thick, sharpened to a blunt point with a knife. A wooden presser – a flat piece of wood fitted with a handle – to prepare seed trays for sowing – can also be made from scrap wood.

Also homemade will be a measuring rod marked in feet and smaller divisions for setting out an outdoor seedbed or planting out at fixed spacings. You will need a garden line, too, to get longer rows straight.

To keep seeds and cuttings moist while they develop, their containers will need to be covered with clear plastic film, supported on wire hoops or with a sheet of glass – or you may prefer to buy containers with purpose-made rigid clear plastic domes. An electric propagator with heating cables set in the base is a further sophistication which will give seeds and cuttings extra encouragement.

Some basic tools will be essential for outdoor cultivation. A border fork – lighter than a full-sized digging fork – is most useful and less tiring to use. A steel rake is needed for levelling and fining the soil for a seedbed. Then you will need a hand-fork and garden trowel for planting.

For watering, you should buy a long-spouted can with a fine rose, suitable for greenhouse and outdoor use. Also a hand sprayer that gives a fine mist to moisten small seeds without washing them out of the soil. A similar sprayer should be kept for combating insect pests with chemicals. You may also need to consider investing in a garden hose and sprinkler to keep seedbeds watered in dry weather.

Equip yourself with a basic selection of pesticides and fungicides to deal with your plants' enemies, not forgetting slug bait to protect succulent seedlings from these voracious pests. Wire netting (or plastic netting) may be necessary to keep off pecking birds too.

Finally, a word of caution: keep all sharp tools, chemicals and plastic bags out of reach of children – preferably locked away when you are not using them.

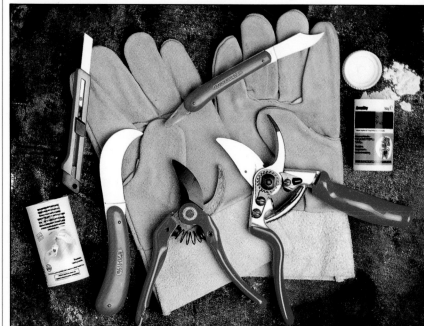

The Right Environment

All plants need the right conditions of light and warmth, moisture, drainage and aeration, shade and food to thrive. The same is true of cuttings and seedlings, except that their needs are more exacting. While thriving mature plants can tolerate a degree of stress from drought, frost or heat, newly propagated material needs to be nursed and protected from all extremes and wide fluctuations if it is to develop and reach a stage where it can fend for itself.

WARMTH

Without sufficient warmth, seeds will not germinate, seedlings will languish and cuttings rot rather than root. It is essential to power the chemical changes that result in rapid cell multiplication and the growth of roots and shoots. But avoid excess or seedlings will be forced into weak lanky growth and probably collapse or shrivel.

Indoor propagating needs something between 60° and 80°F (15° and 27°C), varying with the type of plant, but outdoor demands are less stringent. Hardwood cuttings particularly root in cool conditions.

As important as having the right temperature is maintaining a fairly constant one. Seedlings and cuttings are not resilient enough to tolerate wide fluctuations and likely to die under the strain. The plastic domes or clear plastic film over containers do help to even out temperatures and humidity, and the environment of a heated propagator is largely independent of what goes on around it, making propagating easier and more reliable.

Though I shall consider other environmental factors separately, you need in practice to be able to control and balance them all together, since they all interact and affect each other.

MOISTURE

Water, in the soil and in the atmosphere, is vital to plant growth. It forms much of the substance of plant tissues, it carries plant foods from the soil into and through the plant – since plants really drink, rather than eat – and cools the plant by the process of transpiration as it evaporates from the leaves. Seeds will not germinate without water to swell them and to mobilize the stored food within them. Cuttings will quickly wilt if not kept in high humidity and misted over as often as necessary. Seedlings will collapse and shrivel if they lack water.

But do not 'kill them with kindness'. Too much water will only lead to waterlogging, insufficient oxygen in the soil and trouble from rotting diseases. Gauging the right amount is a matter of careful and frequent observation and above all

A generous mulch keeps tree and shrub roots cool and moist as well as feeding them.

of accumulated experience. Eventually, your plants and seedlings will 'tell' you what they need.

LIGHT

Plant growth will cease without light, since green leaves capture its energy to power their manufacture of carbohydrates and other constituents. So no propagating can succeed without it. Equally, it is vital to protect vulnerable seedlings and cuttings from fierce or hot sun, or they will be scorched. Again, moderation is the key, the exact level being learned by experience. Note that you can have quite high temperatures without fierce light, and that seedlings, for example, will benefit from gradually more light as they develop and strengthen. Nothing operates by a fixed dosage – all is dynamic, changing, yet well balanced for healthy growth.

DRAINAGE

Most plants insist on well-drained soil to thrive. This is because their roots need oxygen as well as water and because stagnant water is a choice breeding ground for fungus diseases that rot plants and stems. So if your geranium cuttings turn black and rotten at the end, look to poor drainage as a prime suspect.

Heavy garden soils and even some mixtures quickly become compacted and hard and airless when frequently watered, as is necessary when propagating. You must water, so you must at the same time improve soil texture and drainage. Add more fibre, such as peat, and more grit (sand, perlite, vermiculite). Plants and cuttings will root in almost pure sand or other gritty material. It pays to start many plants in such a medium, then move them into something more nourishing once they have plenty of roots.

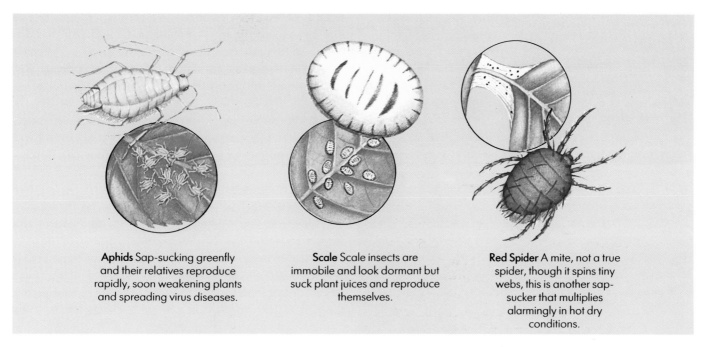

Aphids Sap-sucking greenfly and their relatives reproduce rapidly, soon weakening plants and spreading virus diseases.

Scale Scale insects are immobile and look dormant but suck plant juices and reproduce themselves.

Red Spider A mite, not a true spider, though it spins tiny webs, this is another sap-sucker that multiplies alarmingly in hot dry conditions.

Pests and Diseases

It is essential to propagate only from clean, healthy plants. Clear up any infection from pests or diseases before taking cuttings and discard and burn any plant infected with virus disease, which is incurable. Poor stock is not worth perpetuating and cuttings are far more difficult to treat against infection than the plants they are taken from.

APHIDS, also known as plant lice and greenfly, are all too common and familiar. They congregate on the undersides of plant leaves and on soft fleshy shoot tips, where they suck the sap, weakening the plant. The sticky honeydew they exude can become infected with sooty mould, which is unsightly and stops the leaves breathing and trapping energy from the sun. Aphids can also transmit virus diseases when they feed. Control them by spraying with a permethrin, pyrethrum or dimethoate insecticide, the latter systemic (ie it enters the sap stream of the plant so that the insects are poisoned when they feed).

RED SPIDER MITES are tiny but serious pests that proliferate in hot, dry conditions, and so are discouraged by frequently damping over the plants. They are also sap suckers which turn leaves yellow and speckled. The spider mite's webs form over plants that are badly infested. Control with dimethoate, malathion, pirimiphos-methyl or derris insecticide.

SCALE INSECTS, which suck sap and exude honeydew like aphids, form tiny brown or green blisters on the leaves or stems of some plants, staying mainly stationary. Control with dimethoate (systemic), malathion or permethrin. Watch out for other insect enemies, such as caterpillars, woolly aphids, whitefly or leaf hoppers, which can be controlled with a similar range of chemicals.

SLUGS AND SNAILS can wreak great damage along rows of seedlings or tiny plants, enjoying a succulent nighttime feast. Get in first by defending your 'babies' with a scattering of slug bait (metaldehyde), renewed as necessary.

BIRDS, as mentioned earlier, also relish a little fresh greenery in their diet, so cover young plants with nets or wire-netting when necessary.

DAMPING-OFF is the most serious threat to trays or pots of germinating or pricked-out seedlings. Various fungi attack them at soil level and they turn brown, keel over and die. The infection can spread very rapidly. But if you use a properly sterilized soil mix with a porous, well drained and well aerated texture, your plants are unlikely to suffer. Where you anticipate trouble, spray with Cheshunt Compound or other suitable fungicide.

BLACK LEG is responsible for the failure of many geranium cuttings in late summer. The lower end starts to rot and turns black and the cutting dies. Usually this is the result of overwatering, too low a temperature or choosing too flabby a stem as a cutting. Burn the failures and do better next time!

A cold frame – or a range of them as here, if you need them – is most valuable for overwintering some hardy plants, for hardening off greenhouse-raised plants (getting them used to outdoor conditions gradually) and for taking the overflow from your greenhouse production line, provided the plants concerned are hardy enough. Frames are relatively cheap, keep off wind and heavy rain and lift the temperature a vital degree or two.

GREY MOULD, or botrytis, is a common fungus disease that thrives on damaged or dying tissue and can spread to soft, healthy parts of a plant. It is particularly prevalent in cool, damp stagnant conditions. Control by spraying with benomyl and providing more suitable conditions.

MILDEW shows as a powdery white deposit, which weakens the plant as the fungus feeds upon it. Control with flowers of sulphur or benomyl, a systemic fungicide. Mildew is often encouraged by drought conditions.

HYGIENE Much potential trouble can be avoided by good hygiene. Use only proper sterilized soil mixtures, free from weeds and disease organisms. Remove any dead or dying leaves or flowers, which could soon become host to botrytis. Keep all surrounding areas clean – which includes weed control in the garden and the clearing of rubbish and long grass that can provide a home for slugs, snails, insect pests etc.

Finally, keep all seedlings, cuttings and young plants growing steadily and strongly, without any check to their progress from lack of water, warmth or light. Then they will not easily fall prey to their enemies.

After-Care

Having spent considerable time and effort to get a seed germinated or cutting rooted and growing lustily, it is obviously short-sighted to abandon it to its fate with the minimum of attention. It should rather be adjusted gradually to an independent adult existence and at no time put under more stress than it can bear. Each varies in its requirements, some being quick to establish, others needing a lot of nursing.

Sudden shocks, whether chilling, drought or strong sunshine, will severely check growth and might even result in failure. But with careful observation and frequent attention while moving the plants gradually to cooler, brighter positions, they can gradually be hardened to normal growing conditions. As a plant develops, it will need more food. This will be provided initially by moving it into larger containers of soil mix containing fertilizer, or planting it out in the open – and hopefully fertile – ground. But a regular weak liquid feed will help its progress, ensuring it lacks no particular nutrient and strengthening its resistance to infection.

Some cuttings, particularly of shrubs, tend to grow straight upwards without branching, producing lanky, shapeless plants. It is necessary to nip out their leading shoots at an early stage, so the side buds develop into branches. They will then give you the compact, bushy growth you want.

DIRECTORY OF
PLANT TYPES

Perennials

ACANTHUS SPINOSUS
Bear's Breeches

ZONE 7

This noble thistle-like plant, 4ft (120cm) tall, forms bold spikes of purple-bracted white flowers in late summer, followed by purple-black seeds. Its handsome spiky foliage was widely used as a decorative motif by the Ancient Greeks on their pottery and buildings. Fine as a feature plant, it is easily propagated from seeds, by division or from pieces of its thongy roots.

Seeds should be sown in a greenhouse or on a window-sill at 60°F (15°C) in spring to give them a long season to develop into robust plants by autumn. You could save seeds from your own plants in late summer. Cut the spikes before they can turn mouldy in damp autumn weather and dry off in a greenhouse or indoors. Store them dry and frost-proof until sowing time. Prick out seedlings while young, so their taproots are not damaged. Pot separately in 3½in (8cm) pots and plant out when large enough in early summer.

Lift and divide plants in spring when the temperature reaches about 50°F (10°C). Cut the thick rootstock with a sharp knife or spade. Dust wounds with flowers of sulphur. Plant in well-drained gritty soil – these are Mediterranean plants, used to warmth and dryish soil.

Take root cuttings in late winter. Scrape soil away from one side of a thriving clump and sever one or two pieces of root. Trim these about 2½in (6.5cm) long, straight across the top, slanting at the base to identify which is right way up.

Then insert upright in pots of gritty compost with the top of each cutting level with the surface. If kept moist, but not wet, and moderately warm (50°F/10°C) they will root to form new plants. Once· established, pot separately, then plant outdoors when large enough.

ACHILLEA FILIPENDULINA
Yarrow

ZONES 2–3

This tall (4–5ft/1.2–1.6m) and rather formal border perennial makes a valuable contribution to a summer display, with its flat heads of mustard-yellow flowers which reach almost 6in (15cm) across. It shows up best perhaps with contrasting blue flowers. Besides its use in the garden, its stems can be cut and hung upside down to dry in an airy shed or garage, later to form the centre of some autumn arrangements of dried flowers, brightening the otherwise flower-impoverished months of winter.

Like so many border plants, this one develops spreading clumps of growth which can be carefully divided into several pieces in spring or autumn to make extra plants.

Resembling this achillea but shorter in stature and less stiff in stance are several other achillea species, also propagated by division – notably *Achillea millefolium* 'Cerise Queen', and *A. ptarmica* 'The Pearl'.

Lift agapanthus root in autumn with a garden fork.

Divide fibrous-rooted clump by inserting a fork – or better two forks – and levering apart.

Plant in prepared position where you want it to flower. Set it at same depth as before.

AGAPANTHUS 'HEADBOURNE HYBRIDS'
African Lily

ZONES 8–10

Agapanthus, from Southern Africa, were once thought of as exotic blue lilies resilient enough to stand outdoors in tubs or large pots for the summer while in flower, then to be returned to a greenhouse before autumn could harm them. But now the hardy 'Headbourne Hybrids' can be planted permanently in garden borders in well drained soil in a sunny position and should yield some good clusters of blue or white flowers in mid and late summer. Some climates allow prolific displays, such as those found everywhere by the roadside in Madeira, for instance. This is a common flower of Mediterranean countries and others with a similar climate.

The clumps of stems they form can be carefully broken up in mid- to late-spring and nursed until well established, which will not take long.

ANAPHALIS TRIPLINERVIS
Pearl Everlasting

ZONE 4

This multi-purpose plant is grown first of all for its spreading clumps of silver downy leaves which form a pleasant contrast to green foliage and to flowers of various colours, particularly pink, purple, orange and scarlet. In late summer and early autumn it develops flower stems, also coated in white hairs, which bear papery white flowers. These stems and flowers can be cut and dried off for use with other 'everlastings' in winter decorations indoors.

Anaphalis triplinervis and its close relative, *A. margaritacea,* which has somewhat smaller leaves, grow about 1½ft (45cm) tall. They tolerate most conditions except for heavy, poorly drained soil. It is simplest to divide the clumps of roots to make more new plants. This is another wandering, stoloniferous type of plant, which seems quite a tangle once lifted and broken up. However, every rooted piece will grow, so propagating is easy and reliable. Do this in autumn or spring.

Cut down top growth in autumn, but leave about 15cm (6in) for handling.

Lift clump, with its wandering roots, with a fork.

Divide with the hands or a handfork, cutting any stubborn roots.

Plant healthy new pieces in prepared positions.

Lift clumps when dormant and divide with a fork.

This gives two or more new plants.

ASTER, PERENNIAL
Michaelmas Daisy,
New England Aster

ZONES 2–3

O riginally rather straggly mauve daisies from North America, Michaelmas daisies were developed over many generations to give us extremely showy plants in a generous range of shades and colours on tall or dwarf plants, all characterized by their early autumn flowers. Their main disadvantage is their propensity to mildew, though this can be controlled with a benomyl fungicide, provided you have the time to treat them regularly.

A few good varieties which are less liable to disease are *Aster novae-angliae* 'Alma Potschke' (bright rose; 3½ft/ 105cm), 'Harrington's Pink' (warm pink; 4ft/120cm), 'Autumn Snow' (white; 4½ft/130cm) and the dwarfs *A. novi-belgii* 'Audrey' (mauve-blue; 1ft/30cm), 'Lady in Blue' (10in/25cm), and 'Professor Kippenburg' (clear blue; 1ft/30cm).

Aster amellus varieties such as 'King George' (bright lavender-blue) and 'Brilliant' (bright pink) about 2ft (60cm) tall and *x frikartii* (light lavender blue), 3ft (90cm), tend to be particularly disease-proof.

As with so many perennial border plants, these are all most easily propagated by dividing their clumps of growth in autumn or winter. They vary in vigour and therefore the speed with which they produce suitable material, but are generally obliging.

Space out pieces 25-30cm (10- 12in) apart to form groups of three or five for bold display.

Plant in holes of correct depth in prepared soil.

CHRYSANTHEMUM MAXIMUM
Shasta Daisy

ZONE 4

These magnificent single or double-flowered daisies make a dazzling show from early to late summer in borders or in vases indoors, if you can bear to cut some. In either place, their pure white colouring is a useful foil for other richer-coloured flowers.

A far cry from the dog daisies of our meadows, from which they were developed by Luther Burbank (who named them after Mt. Shasta in California) they form vigorous clumps. These provide the obvious means of making more new plants, since they are easy to divide, either in autumn or spring, and soon become established when planted in nursery rows.

Growing 2½–3ft (75–90cm) high, with blooms 2½–4in (6–10cm) across, these daisies are best acquired as named varieties, like double 'Wirral Pride' or 'Esther Read' or single 'Everest'. It is possible to raise these chrysanthemums from seeds, though the results will not be as fine as you will get from the named varieties, carefully selected over many years.

CAMPANULA PERSICIFOLIA
Peach-leaved Bellflower

ZONE 3

There are many campanulas in a variety of sizes and shapes of bell, but this is one of the best perennial kinds for a border or island bed. Its bells are large and open and borne up the main stems, which can be 2–3ft (60–90cm) tall. They are china blue or white, choice named varieties like 'Telham Beauty' (light blue) and white 'Snowdrift' usually being favoured. These are rather floppy plants that need staking. Slugs love their tasty leaves too, so scatter slug bait as necessary.

This bellflower forms a basal rosette, so it can be carefully divided in autumn or spring to make new plants. Basal cuttings can be taken in late spring or early summer and rooted in gritty soil in a frame as an alternative.

Some good strains of seed are available which will provide you with plants quite easily, though these may not be quite as special as the named varieties. Sow in spring.

CORTADERIA SELLOANA
Pampas Grass

ZONE 8

A clump of Pampas grass with its 18in (45cm) long silvery white plumes can make a striking feature as the centre-piece of a lawn, or set against the background of a dark evergreen hedge. At 8–9ft (2.5–2.8m) high with a spread in proportion to this, you are unlikely to want more than one.

If, however, you want a spare plant for a friend or to start a new clump in some other part of your garden, division of the clump is the method used. This is best done in mid spring. The plumes should be removed in autumn, for decoration indoors before winter winds blow them to pieces. The foliage dies or is very tattered by the spring, so it is usually cut down or even burnt. This is the stage at which to cut and lift sections to make new plants. But be warned: first those leaves have razor-sharp edges, so wear a good pair of gloves; and the clumps will not yield suitable pieces without a struggle. Be sure to get well rooted pieces and nurse them along until you are convinced they have 'taken'.

Cortaderia can also be raised from seeds, sown in spring.

COREOPSIS VERTICILLATA

ZONES 3–9

T his dainty bright yellow daisy flowers from late spring to early autumn, so is particularly good value in the garden. About 1½–2ft (45–60cm) tall, it should be planted in the front rank of a mixed border, or can be used in display beds, so reliable is its show.

It forms a dense fibrous clump of roots, which can be divided in spring or autumn, to give new young plants. It is a really hardy plant, so there is no difficulty about this.

As this is a species, you could sow bought or home-saved seeds in the knowledge that the offspring should be as pleasing as their parents. Start them early under glass or in mid-spring in an outdoor seedbed.

Coreopsis grandiflora and its varieties, such as 'Sunburst' and 'Mayfield Giant' (both 2½ft/75 cm tall) and the dwarf 'Goldfink' (9in/22.5cm high) are taller and showier, though their flowering season is shorter and less continuous. These too can be increased by division.

DELPHINIUM ELATUM
Candle Larkspur

ZONES 2–3

Delphiniums, standing 5–8ft (1.5–2.5m) high, must surely be the noblest and most desirable of all summer border flowers. Their tall spikes of double flowers in a range of blue and purple shades, white and lavender have even earned them a place as specialist hobby flowers.

So how can we make more of these magnificent plants? Fine strains of bought seeds like the Pacific Giants can be sown in early spring and grown on to bloom the following year. But though many delphiniums will set seed in the garden, there is no guarantee that their progeny will be worthwhile, since seedlings from such hybrids tend to revert to inferior forms.

To reproduce a choice variety one has acquired, either divide the clump in spring as it comes into growth after its winter dormancy or root some basal cuttings. The latter are prepared from the young shoots that develop from the root-stock in mid to late spring. Cut them away with a portion of the older tissue and about 2–3in (5–7.5cm) long before their stems become hollow. Trim them if necessary.

Dip them in dilute insecticide solution to ensure they are free from aphids and benomyl fungicide too if it seems necessary to protect them from disease. Then dip the lower ends in rooting hormone and insert in pots of sandy compost and keep them warm and humid until they root, within about three weeks. Pot them individually in 3½in (8cm) pots of more nourishing compost and grow on until they are large enough to plant out. Slugs relish their tender young foliage, so do protect them with slug bait.

ECHINOPS RITRO
Globe Thistle

ZONE 3

This noble plant is grown as much for its handsome deeply lobed foliage and its imposing stature (4–5ft/ 1.2–1.5m) as for its intriguing steel-blue flowers which are clustered in spherical heads 2–3in (5–7.5cm) in diameter. It is most suitable for the back of a border of mixed perennials and its blooms can be cut and dried for winter decoration indoors, provided you do so before the flowers fully open.

The species itself can be raised from seeds sown in spring and results should be pleasing, but there are named forms such as the tall 'Taplow Blue' which must be propagated vegetatively. This is done by dividing the plants in autumn or spring, a method which gives quicker results than seed-sowing anyway. As the roots are fleshy, echinops can also be propagated from root cuttings, in late winter, inserting 3in (7.5cm) lengths of root upright in moist gritty compost. As pieces left in the ground when transplanting will produce new plants unbidden, you can tell it is not likely to be difficult.

ERIGERON HYBRIDS
Fleabane

ZONE 5

The erigerons that are grown in perennial borders and beds are daisies that bear a considerable resemblance to the autumn-flowering asters or Michaelmas daisies; but they are shorter growing at 18in (45cm) and bloom in summer. Developed from native North American flowers, they can play quite a valuable part in the summer garden.

As with so many of our border plants, they are clump forming and so most easily propagated by division in the spring. This is, of course, the only way to perpetuate the choice varieties like pink 'Quakeress' and rich pink semi-double 'Foerster's Liebling'.

Home-saved seeds will not yield reliable results, but a good strain of mixed colours might produce some worthwhile colours. They are easily raised like other perennials in late spring to bloom the following year. Colours are all in the lilac, rose and white range.

EUPHORBIA EPITHYMOIDES (E. POLYCHROMA)
Spurge, Cushion Euphorbia

ZONE 4

This plant has one period of glory each year, when the golden green bracts of its insignificant flowers look as bright if not brighter than many late spring flowers. In fact, though this perennial is generally grown in mixed borders, it is used as a bedding plant in the world-famous Keukenhof Gardens, at Lisse in The Netherlands. Clumps of this euphorbia interplanted with dazzling blue muscari are truly striking. But plant it wherever you need a springtime splash of sunshine.

Related to it are a number of other herbaceous euphorbias. *E. griffithii* 'Fireglow' produces orange bracts in summer and makes a good border plant.

Propagation of these plants is again by division of the clumps of growth. It is best done in spring outdoors. Seeds of the species can be sown in late spring or early summer in the open ground or, in exposed gardens, in a frame.

ERYNGIUM ALPINUM
Sea Holly

ZONE 6

The sea hollies are striking plants with prickly foliage – hence their familiar name – and heads of blue thistle-like flowers. These vary in hue from one to another of the many species. *E. alpinum* has the largest and most handsome flower heads, but the British native *E. maritimum,* which grows in dry sandy soil on the shore, is a worthwhile garden plant too. All these eryngiums thrive in dry gritty soil. Others to look out for are *E. planum* from Eastern Europe, the hybrid *E. x oliverianum* and *E. bourgatii* from the Pyrenees.

Besides the colour and intriguing foliage they bring to a border, they are high on the flower arrangers' list of 'treasures' for displays of character.

Propagation here is from seeds outdoors in late spring or early summer, or from root cuttings in mid winter, for these plants develop fleshy taproots, sections of which will sprout to form new plants. Remove pieces of root about 1½in (4cm) long and insert upright in gritty compost with the top of the cutting at soil level. With a minimum of care they will form shoots and develop into new plants.

GERANIUM ENDRESSII
Hardy Geranium, Endres Cranesbill

ZONE 7

The hardy geraniums, of which this is but one species, form valuable and pleasant-looking ground cover, with the bonus of flowers in late spring. They are European cousins of the bedding geraniums (correctly pelargoniums), which originated in the hotter drier climate of South Africa.

G. endressii is generous with its pink flowers, but a number of others have mauve-blue flowers usually in plenty, 'Johnson's Blue' being a specially lovely one.

Fortunately they can be propagated by division in spring outdoors and form reasonable sized clumps quite quickly. Some species develop thongy roots and sections of these about 1½in (4cm) long can be used as root cuttings in mid winter. Insert them upright in pots of gritty compost, their tops level with the surface. They should form shoots in spring and become usable plants by autumn.

Good strains of seeds are available too and can be sown in an outdoor seedbed in late spring. The results could be mixed, but you should get some worthwhile plants. It should also be possible to collect and sow seeds from your own plants if they ripen before autumn – species only, of course.

HELLEBORUS (CORSICUS) ARGUTIFOLIUS
Corsican Hellebore

ZONE 6

This is a shapely architectural plant, useful as a feature – and better if planted in groups of three or five. In late winter it opens long-lasting clusters of green flowers – more attractive than they sound. These blooms are treasure trove to flower arrangers, so beware scissor-happy ladies!

This hellebore obligingly scatters its seeds about to provide us with self-sown seedlings, so, once you have plants 'propagating' consists of little more than transplanting these seedlings to the positions of your choice.

If you wish to or need to, you can buy a packet of seeds and sow these in spring to start your stock going.

Helleborus orientalis, the Lenten Rose or Lenten Lily, and its many named varieties in a range of colours, which include shades and mixtures of pink, white, maroon and green, is most easily multiplied by division – the only way, of course, to ensure special characteristics are preserved. This is a valuable plant for shady borders and for early spring flowers.

HEMEROCALLIS HYBRIDS
Day Lilies

ZONE 4

Day lilies are vigorous, very hardy plants that form sturdy 2½ft (75cm) high clumps of strap-like leaves and in midsummer clusters of showy flowers in a range of colours. Each bloom lasts but a day, hence their familiar name, but the display continues for several weeks and in some varieties even longer, since there is a generous succession of flowers.

Once rather shunned, as their colour range was limited to yellow and dull orange, hemerocallis now provide us with some exciting red varieties, some with distinctive yellow centres, a wide range of yellows from primrose to the richest of hues. Even green figures in some blooms.

Desirable varieties include 'Stafford', red, 'Pink Damask', 'Golden Chimes', and 'Chartreuse Magic', canary-yellow with green throat.

These plants are very tolerant but do best in moisture retentive soil in full sun or light shade. Being hybrids, they can only be propagated vegetatively and division is the obvious method. Divide their clumps as carefully as you can in spring or autumn. Young vigorous well rooted pieces will soon become established.

IRIS GERMANICA HYBRIDS
Flag Irises

ZONES 5-6

T he common blue flag iris, *I. germanica,* is a hardy, reliable cottage garden flower, while the many choice varieties bred over the years in an almost unbelievable range of colours are less permanent, though their display in early summer is magnificent. They enjoy a position in full sun in well drained, even quite poor soil, where their rhizomes (horizontal stems) can get a good baking and ripening. Their main enemies are waterlogged soil in winter, and slugs and snails, which chew their leaves to pieces.

As hybrids, these choice irises must be propagated vegetatively to ensure that their characteristics are reproduced. Their mode of growth is quite different from the clump-forming perennials and consists of spreading rhizomes or tuberous stems which sit on the surface of the ground, housing the food stores on which they survive the winter.

To make more irises, remove suitable pieces of rhizome, each with a strong fan of leaves and some fibrous roots beneath, and plant these in nursery rows in the open ground. The usual time for this is midsummer, soon after they have flowered, but provided you are prepared to lose the flowers for a season, this could be done as well in autumn or spring. Trim back the fans of leaves by half their length so they lose less moisture while they are rooting and also offer less wind resistance – bearing in mind that their fibrous roots are their only anchorage. They also benefit from lime and bone-meal in the soil, the latter encouraging rooting.

Other rhizomatous irises can be propagated similarly, but there are also fibrous-rooted kinds, notably *Iris sibirica,* which makes more slender plants with somewhat daintier blooms, though it is some 3ft (90cm) high. This is best divided in spring, choosing younger, more vigorous portions from the outer edge of the clump. The winter-flowering *Iris unguicularis (I. stylosa)* is also fibrous-rooted and so can be broken up in the same way to produce more plants to yield those soft mauve orchid-like blooms in the bleak winter days.

Iris foetidissima, the Gladwin, is grown mainly for its pods of orange seeds which burst to look startlingly showy in autumn. They can be cut and used in vases indoors along with the Chinese lanterns and 'Honesty'. Clumps of this iris can be pulled apart and suitable pieces replanted, or it can be raised by sowing the berries in spring. They germinate well to provide you with more than enough seedlings – unless you want a great many for sale or presents. (Incidentally, *I. foetidissima's* strange brownish-claret and gold flowers are really intriguing, if not indisputably beautiful.)

LIRIOPE MUSCARI
Blue Lily Turf

ZONE 6

Some plants are remarkable mimics of other quite different plants. As the second (species) name of this liriope tells us, it looks very much like the bulb, muscari, which edges or carpets many a spring border. The two are in fact distantly related, since they belong to the great lily family, but liriope, from China and Japan, is a fibrous-rooted perennial and its spikes of blue flowers – the main reason for growing it – are at their best in early autumn. There is also a variegated form with leaves striped creamy yellow along their length, forming an effective contrast to the flowers and a cheerful combination of colours.

Propagation is simple, as with many such perennials. Simply lift a thriving clump and pull it apart to provide a number of well rooted pieces, each with some vigorous healthy roots and a good tuft of leaves. If this is done in spring, with a long growing season ahead, and the young plants are well tended until they become re-established there should be no difficulty in making new plants.

LUPINUS POLYPHYLLUS
Lupin, Washington Lupine

ZONE 3

A favourite and colourful border flower, 3–4ft (90–120cm) tall, the lupin is a perennial yet rather short-lived. Originally a North American native, it was transformed in the 1930s by the introduction of Russell's Hybrids with larger flower spikes and a richer range of colours, including bicolors. The dwarf strain 'Lulu' (2–2½ft/60–75cm tall) is useful for small gardens.

To thrive, lupins need well-drained soil, acid rather than alkaline – they become chlorotic on limy soils – and full sun. They are subject to virus infection, so any stunted or sickly looking plants should be lifted and burnt. Slugs enjoy their succulent young foliage, so protect them with slug bait.

To propagate lupins, sow bought seeds, which have been carefully selected to give choice flowers, or perpetuate particular colours by means of basal cuttings. Seeds from your own plants are unlikely to give blooms of a pleasant standard.

Soak seeds in tepid water overnight before sowing to soften their hard seed coats. Raise in seed-sowing mixture at 60°F (15°C) in early spring. Pot up seedlings, then plant out in early summer to flower the following season.

To take basal cuttings, remove sturdy – not thin or flabby – basal shoots about 2in (5cm) long in spring with a small portion of older tissue at the base and insert round the rim of a pot of gritty potting mixture. Kept warm (about 65°F/18°C) and moist they will root to form new plants within three weeks or so. Pot them separately and grown them on steadily. Plant outdoors when large enough and they should bloom well in their second season.

LYSIMACHIA PUNCTATA
Yellow Loosestrife

ZONE 5

W hen in bloom the Yellow Loosestrife is a really showy plant and at the same time very tough and easy to please. It can be fitted into a border of mixed perennials or set in a wild garden with equal success. Reaching about 2½ft (75cm) high, its bright yellow blooms are each set off by claret-coloured stamens. It has every appearance of being a fine cut flower, but practice proves it is quick to drop.

This is a species, so you could raise it from bought or home-saved seeds, sown in early spring and gradually grown on. But its clumps of roots of rather wandering stolon-like growth can easily be divided up to make plenty of new plants, so this remains the favourite method. Such a good-tempered plant can be divided at almost any time during the dormant season, but preferably in autumn or spring.

MENTHA x GENTILIS
Ginger Mint

ZONE 4

Ginger mint is one of a number of mints grown with other perennials for the sake of their decorative foliage, quite independently of any value they may have as aromatic herbs. This one's fresh green leaves are splashed with gold, so a colony of plants can form quite an attractive feature in the front rank of a border. Be warned, though, that like all mints its roots travel to produce new shoots at a short distance from the main plant. Fortunately, ginger mint is reasonably well-behaved and not the threat to garden order posed by the common culinary mint, for instance.

Propagation is, naturally, by dividing up the plants' clumps of roots into smaller pieces to form new colonies, a job best done in early spring. Where many plants are required, or the main clump must be disturbed as little as possible, root cuttings can be used instead. Expose the roots of the plant in early spring without lifting it and remove suitable 1½in (4cm) lengths of root. Lay these horizontally in rooting mixture and keep warm and moist and they should all root and form small new plants.

MONARDA DIDYMA
Bee Balm, Bergamot, Oswego Tea

ZONE 4

Bergamot in its various named varieties can make a colourful contribution to borders in high summer. An aromatic North American plant 2–3ft (60–90cm) high, it was used by the Indians there to make a kind of herb tea. Best varieties are 'Cambridge Scarlet', 'Croftway Pink', 'Snow Maiden' and 'Prairie Night' (purple).

Seed selections are available, but these give a mixture of colours and there is no guarantee what you might get, though it could be worth the gamble.

As with so many perennials, this herbaceous plant makes a spreading clump, so can readily be divided into smaller pieces – in autumn or in spring. They will soon become established, though it is as well to bear in mind that this plant likes a moist soil, preferably near water. This is a good display plant which deserves to be more widely featured in gardens.

Lift tuberous-rooted paeony root carefully while plant is dormant.

PAEONY, HERBACEOUS
Peony

ZONES 3 – 4

Paeonies are probably the most sumptuous of all the old cottage garden flowers, with heavy double blooms and handsome shapely foliage which often turns beautiful red and purple shades before finally withering in the autumn. Their one great disadvantage is their brief season of some two weeks or a little more, related to the amount of space they take up. A border or large bed filled with paeonies can be a thrilling sight in early summer but just boring the rest of the year. Consequently, they are best planted among other flowers which continue the display of colour.

But having acquired a pink 'Sarah Bernhardt' or a *P. officinalis* 'Rubra Plena', how can one make more plants? The answer is by division, but with a difference. Paeonies grow from tuberous roots, so each section that is destined to make a new plant must consist of at least one strong healthy tuber and one or two fat scarlet buds at soil level.

Division is done in early spring before the foliage appears but just when there is a surge of vigour and fresh root development is most likely. This task is not difficult, but paeonies have a reputation for resenting disturbance, so you will probably have to be patient for a couple of years before seeing flowers again. This is a gross feeder too, so plant the new plants in well-fed ground, including rotted manure.

Divide with a sharp knife. Make sure each piece has basal buds and adequate roots.

Replant the separate sections immediately so they do not dry out.

35

PHALARIS ARUNDINACEA 'PICTA'
Gardener's Garters, Ribbon Grass

ZONE 3

If you have ever had to struggle with an infestation of couch grass (*Agropyron* sp.), with its questing white roots which seem to penetrate into everything and of which the tiniest broken fragment roots to make a new plant, you may be rather cautious with this variegated grass. But it is not as vigorous as couch and certainly makes a smart clump of stripy leaves in the front rank of a mixed border. Stems can be picked and added to vases of flowers too. With care, you can cut round the edge of an established clump with a sharp spade periodically and remove all the unwanted pieces.

Propagation is, of course, by division. As already explained, pieces of the stolons or wandering roots will produce new plants. The job is perhaps best done in spring, but as this is a tough sort of plant, it could be done at other times, except when the weather is extreme, with every likelihood of success.

PHYGELIUS CAPENSIS
Cape Fuchsia

ZONE 7

This colourful plant is not as widely known as it deserves, since it is no trouble and once established gives a good late summer display of orange-scarlet blooms on 2½–3ft (75–90cm) high plants. Though it bears a close resemblance to some kinds of fuchsia, it is not in fact related to them. There are related kinds with yellow or pink flowers too.

Phygelius spreads by means of running underground stems which give rise to suckering shoots. These, of course, are a ready means of propagation in spring. When lifting pieces for propagating, note that these stems can become rather tangled so you may need to lift more of your plant than you intended.

Seeds are available and can be sown in spring in pans in a greenhouse. It is also possible to root semi-hardwood cuttings in a gritty mix in a greenhouse during the middle of the summer.

PHYSALIS ALKEKENGI
Chinese Lanterns

ZONES 2–3

This old favourite is nothing to look at when in flower in a border, with small rather plain white flowers, followed by greenish seed capsules, but when the latter turn a rich orange it is a different matter. They can be showy in the garden and are keenly sought by flower arrangers too. Cut and dried off, they make superb winter decorations indoors, particularly mixed with the silver seed heads of 'Honesty' *(Lunaria)*.

Be warned, this is not just a spreading plant, but a wanderer, even a trespasser, so plant it preferably in some rather out of the way part of the garden. It loves full sun but is not fussy about soil type.

It is simple to lift and divide some of its wandering roots to make more new plants – either in autumn or spring. Planted in moist soil, they will quickly establish and romp into growth.

If you wish to, or need to, you can raise this plant from seed, sown in spring in pots or in a seedbed outdoors and transplanted when large enough. Again, they are no trouble.

PHYSOSTEGIA VIRGINIANA
Obedient Plant,
Virginia Lionsheart

ZONES 2–3

This perennial, an 2–2½ft (60–75cm) tall plant, is particularly valued for its early autumn display, which comes at a time when so many perennial border plants have passed over. A good accompaniment for *Colchicum autumnale*. Apart from the pink-flowered species, 'Vivid' is a choice rose-coloured variety and 'Summer Snow' a pleasing white. Physostegia is happy in sun or semi-shade in moist soil.

This is a travelling plant with stoloniferous roots which send up flowering stems at a short distance from the main clump of the plant. However, it cannot be said to be other than well-behaved. Its familiar name of Obedient Plant refers however, to the individual flowers on its spikes, which will stay where they have been pushed if you care to try doing this.

Propagation of this plant is, as you would expect, easiest by division – and, of course, essential to maintain the special characteristics of the named varieties. But it can also be raised from bought seeds in spring, if you wish, to give acceptable flowers.

PYRETHRUM
Painted Daisy

ZONES 2–3

These much-loved summer flowers, widely marketed as cut flowers as well as having a valuable role in the garden, are basically red chrysanthemums, correctly known as *C. coccineum*. They are not unlike the white Shasta daisies.

A number of choice named varieties are grown, including single pink 'E.M. Robinson', single crimson 'Bressingham Red', and rich maroon-red 'Brenda'. 'Vanessa' (pink) and 'Lord Rosebery' (red) are double-flowered.

Pyrethrums are a little more choosy than most perennials, calling for well-drained fertile soil. As they are not as tough as some plants, confine dividing them to warmer times of year – either in spring as they come into growth, or just after their early to midsummer flowers are over. This is easily done, though you may be glad to use a knife to cut cleanly through the tough clumps of roots.

It is possible to raise pyrethrums from good seed mixtures, but of course there is no guarantee what colours you will get in this way. All named hybrids must be increased by division.

SALVIA x SUPERBA
Sage

ZONE 5

This form of perennial sage is fine for contributing some rich purple-blue colouring to a planting of perennials, which could be a long bed or an oval or kidney-shaped bed. The species itself is quite vigorous, making a plant 3ft (90cm) tall. But recently the accent has been on developing shorter more compact plants for patios or modest-sized gardens. 'East Friesland' is the variety to look for here, being only 1½ft (45cm) high and needing no staking – a time saver. 'Purple Glory' is a taller variety which can reach 3ft (90cm).

This is yet another clump-forming plant that can be divided in spring or autumn, though it is far less vigorous than the asters and *Chrysanthemum maximum*, so material for propagating will not be so plentiful. The process itself, however, is as straightforward as ever.

SEDUM SPECTABILE
Stonecrop, Ice Plant,
Showy Sedum

ZONE 3

The most remarkable feature of this plant is that its flowers are favourites for both bees and butterflies. When in bloom in late summer and early autumn it attracts many species of butterfly and at the same time may be buzzing with honey bees.

This 1–2ft (30–60cm) tall plant forms rosettes of icy blue-green leaves covered in a whitish bloom. Then in late summer it develops tallish flower stems, each carrying a flat cluster of many tiny flowers, usually red or pink in colour.

Showy in bloom, it can be used as a path edging or set in a suitable position on a rock garden. Fine varieties include 'Brilliant' and 'Meteor', both rich pink, and also 'Autumn Cheer' a hybrid with *S. telephium* which develops longer stems and larger flower clusters which open salmon-pink then turn a rusty red as they age.

It pays to plant these carefully selected varieties, so propagation must be from parts of mature plants and division is the obvious technique. This is quite straightforward and can be done in autumn or spring.

SIDALCEA MALVAEFLORA
Prairie Mallow,
Foothill Checkermallow

ZONE 8

This dainty cousin of the familiar hollyhock is tougher than it looks and is a most prolific flowerer in mid to late summer. Why is it not more widely planted, I wonder? Its blooms are generally of some shade of pink, varying from the shell-pink of 'Loveliness' via 'Rose Queen' to salmon 'William Smith', respectively 2½ft (75cm), 4ft (1.2m) and 3ft (90cm) high. A good middle-of-the-border plant, this sidalcea well earns its keep so should be on every gardener's order list. Stake it early in the season, so that wind and rain cannot smash down its stems.

This is a remarkably tolerant plant, happy in most soils provided they don't get dry, which is the main danger. Division is again the best method to make more new plants and essential if you want more of the named varieties. Do this in spring and they will soon develop new roots to become strong independent plants.

STACHYS LANATA
Lamb's Ears

ZONE 4

This spreading woolly silver-leaved ground covering plant is another of the dead nettle family. Its flowers are more of a curiosity, however, than a decoration, so gardeners generally remove them to enjoy the undisturbed beauty of the silver leaves. There is, indeed, a non-flowering selection called 'Silver Carpet'.

Most often used as an edging plant, *Stachys lanata* can be used for carpet planting in summer displays setting off bright purple verbena, scarlet salvia, rich orange-yellow gazania or various pink flowers with equal success.

Division is a simple and straightforward way of making more plants in autumn or spring – or at almost any time in pleasant weather. The pieces will soon become established. If any fragments should die back, just cut or pull them out.

The species itself can also be raised from seeds, including those from your own plants, but the specially selected 'Silver Carpet' can only be multiplied vegetatively.

TRADESCANTIA VIRGINIANA
Spiderwort

ZONE 4

This 1½–2ft (45–60cm) high summer border flower is particularly intriguing, since its prolific clusters of flowers boast only three petals apiece, quite a rare occurrence among flowers. While the species is a pleasant mid-blue, a number of choice varieties in various colours are offered for gardens. 'Isis' is a particularly good royal blue with larger flowers than the species, 'Osprey' a white with distinctive blue stamens which give it an orchid-like appearance, while 'J.G. Weguelin' is pale blue and 'Purewell Giant' carmine. It prefers moist soil and partial shade.

It forms vigorous spreading clumps, so is most readily propagated by division in autumn or spring. While the named varieties must be perpetuated in this way, bought seed selections can provide a mixture of acceptable flowers. Sow them in spring, as for other border perennials.

VERONICA TEUCRIUM
'Crater Lake Blue'

ZONE 3

This veronica and its cousin *V. incana,* which is rather similar except that its leaves are grey and downy rather than green, is a modest-growing plant little over 1ft (30cm) tall. But its spikes of blue or pink flowers earn it a place in the front rank of a mixed border.

These plants can be raised from seed mixtures, though, of course, you will not then benefit from the careful selection that produced named forms like pink 'Barcarolle' or 'Blue Spire'. Sow them in mid or late spring so they develop into strong plants by autumn and then overwinter to bloom the next season.

The plants form loose clumps of growth which can be carefully divided in spring, making sure that each piece has adequate fibrous roots and some healthy shoots. Nurse them along until they get well established.

It is possible to take softwood stem cuttings about 2–2½in (5–7.5cm) long from the plants in late spring or early summer and root these in pots in a greenhouse or frame.

Shrubs

BUDDLEIA DAVIDII
Butterfly Bush

ZONE 5

This large shrub is probably better known for the butter-flies that sip its nectar than for its purple flowers. It is certainly a showy and easy plant, making 4ft (1.2m) of new growth in a season and surviving the hardest of winters. Do not be satisfied with any pale mauve buddleia, unless you particularly fancy this hue. Look for rich purple 'Royal Red', 'White Profusion' or 'Harlequin' a purple-flowered variety with variegated leaves.

Propagation is simple enough from hardwood cuttings taken in early autumn and inserted in a sheltered part of the garden. Take well ripened shoots of the current year's growth, about 1ft (30cm) long, trim them beneath a leaf joint and remove any soft tip growth. They should root by spring. Buddleias can be rooted from softwood cuttings in a greenhouse in spring. Good seed selections are offered.

Select well-ripened shoots of current year's growth in autumn for use as hardwood cuttings.

Leaf bud cuttings

Select a healthy shoot of current year's growth in late summer.

Cut across just above each leaf bud.

Typical prepared leaf-bud cutting.

Dip each cutting in hormone preparation to encourage rooting.

Insert cuttings round rim of pot of gritty mixture. Keep close until rooted.

CAMELLIA JAPONICA

ZONE 7

Camellias must be among the most aristocratic of all flowering shrubs, with their stiff shiny evergreen foliage and almost too perfectly formal blooms. Grown in a cool greenhouse or conservatory where they are protected from frost, which rarely harms the bushes but can sadly mar their flowers, they look magnificent. Outdoors, you take risks with them, as so often their blooms are browned by cold winds or frost just as they reach perfection.

Most camellias grown in gardens are choice hybrids, so seeds are not a suitable means of propagation, but several kinds of cuttings can be used. First of them, leaf bud cuttings, taken in late summer in a greenhouse with bottom heat of 65–70°F (18–21°C). Use lengths of stem ½–1in (1.3–2.5cm) long, cut just above a leaf (with the essential bud at its base) and some way beneath it. Treat with hormone rooting preparation and insert in a sand/peat rooting medium. Bottom heat is essential to root camellias. It will become obvious that the cuttings have rooted when there is fresh growth.

Semi-hardwood cuttings can be taken in much the same way in late summer, though the cuttings will, of course, be longer with several leaf buds apiece.

If there are suitable low-growing branches or shoots, ripe shoots can be wounded near a leaf joint, by cutting diagonally part way through, the wound propped open with a sliver of wood, then covered with a layer of old soil-based potting mix to encourage roots. Peg the shoot into the ground to keep it steady and stake the end of the shoot upright with a cane so that it produces a shapely new plant. This can be severed from the parent when it is well rooted, usually in the spring of its second season. Shoots can be layered from mid spring to late summer. The cost of camellia plants makes propagation worthwhile.

Half-ripe stem cuttings

Select a healthy current year's shoot when half-ripe. Strip away lower leaves.

Cut across just under leaf joint to make a cutting about 10cm (4in) long.

Insert against the rim of a pot of gritty compost and keep close until it roots.

CARYOPTERIS x CLANDONENSIS
Blue Spiraea, Bluebeard

ZONE 5

This is a particularly valuable blue-flowered shrub, which flowers in early autumn after most shrub flowers are over. With somewhat silvered hairy foliage it is pleasant when not in flower too. Developed from wild species from the colder northern parts of China, it is certainly very hardy. It does, however, tend to grow rather straggly unless pruned back quite hard in early spring each year.

Cuttings provide the best way of propagating it – preferably semi-hardwood ones taken during the summer in pots in a greenhouse. Softwood cuttings taken in spring are an alternative.

The colour quality of the flowers can vary quite widely, so it pays to choose a choice variety like 'Kew Blue' which is quite rich in colouring.

CORNUS ALBA 'SIBIRICA'
Red-stemmed Dogwood, Siberian Dogwood

ZONE 2

A number of selected forms of *Cornus alba* are grown for their decorative effect in gardens. Their deep wine-red stems are their main claim to a place, but many also take on pleasant if not startling autumn tints in early autumn which make a valued contribution to the scene. The variegated forms 'Elegantissima' (white-edged leaves) and 'Spaethii' (green and gold) also contribute interesting leaf colour from spring to autumn, though the latter's stems are less spectacular.

Several methods of propagation are used to multiply these shrubs. Seeds (of species only) can be sown in spring in a greenhouse or frame though this is a rather slower way than using part of the parent plant. Where this forms suckers, one or two of these can be carefully lifted and severed to make new plants. Layering is another rather similar means. Just pin low-growing branches into the soil, after wounding them where roots are required. They should oblige within a few weeks, but leave them for some months to become established before severing and lifting them.

Hardwood cuttings, taken in early autumn and inserted in a sheltered part of the garden, form another straightforward way of acquiring new plants. With so many choices, it should not be difficult to form a weed smothering plantation of them, or a decorative screen to keep out prying eyes.

COTONEASTER HORIZONTALIS
Herringbone Cotoneaster, Rock Spray

ZONE 4

The most familiar of the many species of cotoneaster planted in gardens, this one is generally set against a wall or in some place where its flat growth will carpet the ground and cascade over a low wall or the edge of a pool. Its fascinating herringbone growth is clothed in shiny green leaves from spring to autumn, and they turn a rich fiery red before falling. Myriads of tiny white flowers in early summer are followed by scarlet berries in late summer and autumn.

The most literal way of getting 'plants for free' is to lift seedlings that have arisen near the plant with a hand-fork. Their roots will be longer than you expected. If you are not favoured with such seedlings, you can sow some of the plant's own seeds in spring, after stratifying them through the winter to break their dormancy (see Introduction on Methods of Propagation).

Where branches touch the ground, they can form roots and such natural 'layers' can be lifted and severed to form new plants. Or you can coax branches to root in this way by wounding them and pinning them down in the soil.

Finally, you can root semi-hardwood cuttings in pots in a greenhouse in late summer/early autumn. These methods are also used to propagate other cotoneasters which you may have in your plant collection.

CYTISUS SCOPARIUS
Common Broom, Scotch Broom

ZONE 5

Common broom is a picture when bearing masses of its bright yellow flowers against a background of blue sky and puffs of white cloud and is quite eligible for the garden as·well as wild areas. But there are a number of variously coloured forms which add to its interest. 'Andreanus', for example, is also marked with brownish crimson, some forms are white or cream-yellow, others introduce wine-red shades. Flowering time is late spring.

Seeds are probably the best means of propagation, though the special forms will be something of a gamble. You will not know what colours you have until they flower in their second year. Note that brooms make taproots which resent being broken so seedlings should be moved on into larger pots as necessary to accommodate them, until it is time to plant them out.

To perpetuate choice colours and be sure of them, take semi-hardwood cuttings in late summer, inserted in pots of gritty soil mix in a greenhouse (or on a windowsill).

DEUTZIA GRACILIS
Slender Deutzia

ZONE 4

This is but one of a number of species of deutzia, many of them from Japan, plus a number of fine hybrids largely produced by the Lemoine nursery in France, but it is particularly elegant, both as a garden shrub and as a potted shrub, smothered in dainty white bells in spring.

While *D. gracilis* bears only white flowers, others of this genus have pink or purple-pink bells. At 4–6ft (1.2–2m) tall, they are useful for the middle rank of a shrub border and always attract attention when in flower.

Propagation is simple – either semi-hardwood cuttings during the summer in a frame, or hardwood cuttings similarly in mid winter. Once you have this particularly lovely shrub, you are sure to want a few extras to try in pots or give away as presents.

Euonymus fortunei radicans 'Variegatus'.

Euonymus fortunei radicans 'Emerald 'n' Gold'.

EUONYMUS FORTUNEI
'SILVER QUEEN'

ZONE 5

Formerly known as *E. radicans,* after its trailing rooting-as-it-goes habit, this variegated shrub is most useful and decorative as an edging to a path or, planted on a larger scale, as ground cover. Once well established it blankets out weeds effectively. If planted against a wall it will start to climb and can reach 2–3ft (60–90cm) up the wall – quite ornamental!

Look out for other forms too, like 'Emerald 'n' Gold', with, as its name indicates, green and gold leaves.

Propagation is quite simple – just a matter of dividing up thriving clumps in spring and setting out well rooted pieces in nursery rows to grow on to a size suitable to plant in selected permanent positions, though if you do not mind the temporary bareness you could put them straight in their final positions.

EUONYMUS JAPONICUS 'AUREOVARIEGATUS'

ZONE 7

This is a particularly attractive variegated evergreen shrub, far superior to the original green-leaved form, which is sometimes used for hedging and screening by the sea. It forms a densely branched hummock of branches of rather lax growth, reaching perhaps 4ft (1.2m) high but 6ft (2m) or more across. Cheerful at all times of year, it does, however, need good sunshine to retain its variegation.

This valuable ornamental plant can be propagated from semi-hardwood cuttings in late summer or early autumn – outdoors if this is done early, otherwise in a frame or in pots of gritty mix, after dipping suitable side shoots in rooting hormone.

Such a lax growing shrub could also provide suitable branches for layering and these can be wounded and pinned into the soil to root. Lift and sever them when they have formed sufficient roots to fend for themselves.

Select suitably ripened shoot in autumn for use as a hardwood cutting.

FORSYTHIA x INTERMEDIA 'SPECTABILIS'

ZONE 4

This much loved spring-flowering shrub is so widely grown in gardens now as to colour the landscape with its sunny yellow flowers. But when planting it, do give thought to the fact that once its flowers are over it is no more attractive than privet. So plant it among other shrubs that flower later, or in a position where it will not monopolize the view in later spring and summer.

'Spectabilis' is an outstanding form with large and plentiful blooms. 'Suspensa', as its name implies, is of arching, almost weeping growth and naturally layers some of its lower branches, which can then be lifted and severed ready to plant elsewhere. 'Beatrix Farrand' is a fine American hybrid raised at the Arnold Arboretum, while 'Bronxensis' is a generous-flowering dwarf only about 2ft (60cm) high, for the rock garden.

Apart from layering where suitable, forsythias can be rooted from semi-hardwood cuttings in late summer or hardwood cuttings in mid autumn. Such a vigorous shrub is not difficult to root.

50

Select a half-ripe shoot, in late summer to provide a cutting.

Prepare cutting by stripping lower leaves and cutting across just under a leaf joint.

Insert against the rim of a pot of gritty compost.

FUCHSIA MAGELLANICA 'GRACILIS'
Magellan Fuchsia

ZONE 6

Fuchsias with their dainty swinging ballet-skirted blooms are extremely popular as summer pot plants. They can be set outdoors during the warmer months of the year, but very few are hardy enough to survive a frost. *Fuchsia magellanica,* however, can be planted outdoors and though its aerial growth may be cut back by winter's frosts and searing winds, it will usually sprout afresh from the base in spring to produce a bushy plant some 4–5ft (1.2–1.5m) high by mid-summer when it is smothered in blooms. It was always one of the old cottage garden favourites.

Once you have enjoyed this delightful plant, you will want more, either to enjoy in other parts of your garden or to pass on to friends. Softwood or semi-hardwood cuttings are the way to provide for this, the former in spring, the latter during the summer, as the stems start to ripen and lignify.

Select a suitable sideshoot of soft growth in early summer.

Prepared cutting inserted by the rim of a pot of gritty mixture.

HEBE PINGUIFOLIA 'PAGEI'
Shrubby Veronica

ZONE 5

This small ground-hugging shrub is valued for the colour of its small blue-grey leaves and also for its weed-smothering propensities. While it can be used as a single specimen or along with other plants to edge a path, as a ground coverer it will show up the more spectacularly if set off by adjoining colonies of purple-leaved ajuga (*Ajuga reptans* 'Atropurpurea') for instance, or golden creeping Jenny (*Lysimachia nummularia* 'Aurea').

This hebe can be encouraged to form layers merely by earthing over some of its prostrate branches. There should not be any need to wound them or use rooting hormone, but this would make success more certain.

Larger numbers of youngsters can be produced from cuttings – either 1½in (4cm) long softwood cuttings in spring or early summer or 2–2½in (5–7.5cm) long semi-hardwood ones later between midsummer and mid autumn. This is the easiest way to turn a specimen plant into a ground-covering colony.

HYDRANGEA HORTENSIS
Hydrangea

ZONES 5–6

Hydrangeas are planted widely in some places for their long and reliable summer display, above all, perhaps, by the sea in milder areas. The colour of their flower heads varies considerably according to the chemical composition of the soil in which they are growing, the sought-after blues coming only on acid soils. Limy soils will give red or purple flowers.

If you are not content with the results nature gives you on your soil, then grow some in tubs and provide them with the kind of compost they need. Dosing with hydrangea colourant also helps – it is usually based on alum. My point is to warn you before you are disappointed that if you take a cutting from a friend's ethereal blue hydrangea, root it and plant it in your own limy soil, you will not enjoy that same blue at all! So resort to tubs, as I have suggested.

But semi-hardwood cuttings are easy to root in pots in the greenhouse in midsummer, or outdoors in late summer, provided you do not allow them to wilt in hot sun and lose too much water. Shade them and reduce the size of each mature leaf on the cuttings by half.

Also widely grown as a houseplant for winter flower.

HYPERICUM CALYCINUM
Aarons Beard, St John's Wort

ZONE 6

This large-flowered St John's wort, at its best in high summer, makes spreading carpet-like growths which smother out all weeds. It therefore makes effective and reasonably neat ground cover. Its cascading habit suits it well to clothing banks, avoiding the chore of frequent mowing or clipping of grass, and it will also thrive in the dry soil round the bases of trees, though it is likely to flower less well if there is any density of shade.

Its spreading habit of growth and the fact that it roots as it goes mean that it is easy enough to lift rooted pieces, preferably in autumn or early spring, to form new plants. This hypericum can also be raised from seeds – slower, but it does develop fairly speedily.

The more conventional shrubby *H. patulum,* in its choice form 'Hidcote', perhaps, is best perpetuated by means of semi-hardwood cuttings in a frame in early autumn. It flowers for several weeks.

KOLKWITZIA AMABILIS
Beauty Bush

ZONE 4

The Beauty Bush well deserves its name because of the flurry of charming little pink blooms it sports in early summer. It is somewhat like a weigela, though daintier. Widely grown in America, it is a flowering shrub that deserves greater popularity in Europe. As it is deciduous and rather straggly looking when leafless, plant among evergreens.

Growing some 5ft (1.5m) tall, it is suitable for the middle rank of a full-scale shrub border. To make more plants, it is necessary to use semi-hardwood cuttings and root them in mid to late summer in a frame or greenhouse.

LIGUSTRUM OVALIFOLIUM 'AUREUM'
Golden Privet,
California Privet

ZONE 5

Privet in its green-leaved form is widely used as a hedging plant and whatever one's reservations about it as regards over-vigorous growth, frequency of cutting necessary and voracious roots robbing our borders of plant foods and moisture, it remains a most useful plant. Its golden-leaved form 'Aureum' is altogether more refined, if less vigorous, though quite adequate growth, and truly decorative. In fact, I have seen a free-standing bush of this at a distance in winter and thought it was forsythia in full bloom. Its golden foliage is always cheerful – such a benefit in a cloudy climate – and it can be grown as an ornamental foliage shrub or used for a decorative hedge.

Propagation – of necessity vegetative to pass on its special colouring – is simple enough from hardwood cuttings taken in mid autumn and inserted in a sheltered part of the garden. Most should root by spring, but do not be in a hurry to lift and transplant them. Wait until they have strong roots.

LONICERA NITIDA 'BAGGESEN'S GOLD'
Box Honeysuckle

ZONE 7

The original green-leaved species, *L. nitida,* is often planted to form a neat hedge with its tiny glossy dark green leaves. It takes well to clipping but needs only one haircut a year. 'Baggesen's Gold' (so often misspelt!) is a cheerful golden form which can, like golden privet, be grown as a free-standing shrub or clipped to form a small hedge. While it is duller in colour in winter, it still makes a cheerful feature then.

It is quite easy to root from hardwood cuttings in mid autumn. Just strip away suitable sideshoots with a heel of older growth and insert in a slit trench in a suitably prepared part of the garden. I have also found that mature bushes can layer themselves into the soil, providing ready made youngsters which only need severing from their parent.

MAHONIA AQUIFOLIUM
Oregon Grape

ZONE 5

This North American shrub is both very hardy and ever-green, as well as being quite showy when in flower in early spring and later when bearing its clusters of blue-bloomed black grape-like berries. As for its role in the garden, it can be grown as a free-standing shrub, planted in groups to form an informal screen or flowering hedge, and even used for ground cover.

As this useful shrub spreads by means of suckering growths, these can be carefully lifted, severed from their parent and planted elsewhere to grow on – preferably during spring when growth is most vigorous. Birds love mahonia berries and after eating them void the seeds to give us plenty of self-sown seedlings, which can be carefully lifted and grown on.

A similar plant of better value as a decorative plant is the hybrid 'Charity', which blooms off and on from mid autumn to late winter. It makes a taller shrub, upright in habit. Another is 'Undulata', whose shiny evergreen leaves have wavy edges.

Select semi-ripe sideshoot for use as cutting. Your oleander may be growing outdoors.

Cut just beneath a leaf joint to give a cutting about 10cm (4in) long.

To prepare cutting strip away all lower leaves and cut off just under third leaf joint from the top.

NERIUM OLEANDER
Oleander

ZONES 7–8

The oleander is only suitable for warm frost-free gardens, such as those in California and the Southern states of the USA, but elsewhere is an easy conservatory plant, needing little more than freedom from frost. A minimum of about 43°F (6°C) will suit it well. Quite a vigorous shrub, growing about 6–8ft (1.8–2.5m) high, it flowers generously through the summer. While its blooms are most commonly rose-pink, there are also white and peach and red forms, and doubles as well as singles.

To make more oleanders and to perpetuate the special colour forms, take semi-hardwood cuttings in late summer or early autumn. These will, in fact, root in water as well as in pots of gritty mix, though care must then be taken when potting them up as such roots are notoriously soft and brittle.

Seeds offer another means of propagation. Sow a reliable seed mixture in spring in warmth and you should get some worthwhile plants. However, you will then have to wait perhaps two years for them to mature and bloom before you know what colours they are.

Spread sand over top of compost in pot so some trickles into hole made for cutting.

Make a hole against the rim with a small dibber.

Insert cutting close to side of pot where it is more likely to root.

RIBES SANGUINEUM
Flowering Currant, Winter Currant

ZONE 5

A cousin of our edible red and black currants, this very hardy flowering shrub from the western side of North America is widely planted and easy to grow, though not to be shunned as 'ordinary'. The only precaution is to choose a well-coloured form, since some are very weak washed-out pink. Choose a rich pink like 'Carneum' or a red shade like 'Pulborough Scarlet' or 'King Edward VII'. 'Album' has white flowers and 'Brocklebankii' is unusual on account of its golden foliage.

It is an early flowerer, starting to open with the first of the forsythias in late winter or early spring. In fact, I have photographed it with snow on its flower clusters.

It is most readily propagated from hardwood cuttings taken in late autumn or early winter either outdoors or in a frame – the latter particularly where winters are harsh.

———————

Choose a suitably ripened shoot of current year's growth to make a hardwood cutting.

ROSES

ZONES 3–7

R oses are, of course, among the best loved of all garden flowers and so particularly worth propagating. But those most often grown, for their individual beauty and for the massed colour they can contribute to the garden in summer, are hybrids produced by budding the desired variety on to a vigorous rootstock.

While it is possible to root some of these varieties from hardwood cuttings inserted outdoors in early winter in the normal way, results can be unreliable, since the reason for budding is to give them the greater vigour of the rootstock, such as the wild *Rosa canina*. Without that rootstock they could prove weak, flower sparsely and have a shorter life. There is nothing lost, however, when shortening the bushes in autumn to use some of the prunings as cuttings and await results.

Rambler roses and other strong-growing kinds are a safer proposition from hardwood cuttings.

Seeds of species roses – the grey-purple-leaved *Rosa rubrifolia*, for example, comes to mind – can be started from seeds sown in the spring. The hips, collected in the autumn, must first be stratified (spread between layers of sharp sand in a pot or aerated box protected from hungry vermin and stood at the base of a cold north wall for the winter to break the seeds' dormancy).

———————

LEFT 'Just Joey'
ABOVE 'Charles Dickens'

Sambucus racemosa 'Plumosa Aurea'.

SAMBUCUS NIGRA 'AUREA'
European Elder, Golden Elder

ZONE 5

The wild elderberry yields heavy clusters of white flowers in early summer, which are often collected to make wine. These are followed by shiny black fruits, which can be used to make a preserve, or again wine. But in gardens this over-vigorous unpleasant-smelling shrub or small tree is not normally tolerated. But it has yielded several ornamental forms, of which the golden elder is probably the most highly valued. To encourage it to bear plenty of its sunny leaves and at the same time restrict its height and spread, it is generally pruned hard back to within 1–1½ft (30–45cm) of the ground each year in early spring, so it consists largely of young wood.

This choice form is easily propagated from semi-hardwood cuttings in a greenhouse in mid to late summer or from hardwood cuttings in a frame or even the open ground in late autumn/early winter. Such a vigorous grower generally obliges by rooting quite readily.

SANTOLINA CHAMAECYPARISSUS
Cotton Lavender

ZONES 6–7

This neat silver shrublet can prove quite versatile in the garden. It will grow into a sprawling mound 3ft (90cm) across and 2½ft (75cm) high, against which its many golden button flowers show up splendidly in midsummer – unless you feel they detract from its silver effect and decide to snip them off. It can also form a dwarf dividing hedge about 2ft (60cm) high, taking kindly to restrictive clipping. As its foliage is aromatic, it is also planted in herb gardens and gardens for the blind, where it is generally set in a raised bed where its foliage can be fingered.

Propagation is simple – from hardwood cuttings stripped away with a heel of older growth in early winter and inserted in the open ground. Similar cuttings can be taken in early autumn when they are still semi-ripe and inserted round the rims of pots of gritty mixture and housed in frames or a cool greenhouse until they root.

Select santolina shoot, woody at the base. Strip off all lower leaves and trim heel.

Prepare slit trench with sharp sand in bottom to take a row of cuttings buried to two-thirds depth.

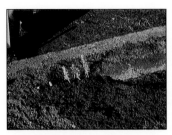

Insert cuttings along vertical side of slit trench, about 7.5cm (3in) apart.

Refill trench with soil.

Firm soil against base of cuttings to encourage rooting.

SENECIO LAXIFOLIUS·

ZONE 5

This silver-leaved shrub from New Zealand has become popular in recent years for its foliage colour – not only in shrub borders but in the flower arranger's hands for indoor decoration too. Its generous clusters of bright yellow daisies in midsummer contrast boldly with its overall silver hue – and, if planned ahead, with blue flowers like delphiniums. However, many gardeners see them as a distraction from the silver effect and as rather too brash to leave alone, so they snip them off before they can 'shout'.

This qualification apart, it is a most valuable garden shrub, which also forms rather arching growth, so is an ideal candidate for planting at the top of a bank or low wall.

This shrub's lowest branches will often root into the soil, providing the gardener with some natural 'layers'. These can be severed and lifted when rooted well and transplanted where they are required.

Semi-hardwood cuttings can be rooted in early autumn, following the same technique as used for bedding geraniums (pelargoniums), though, of course, their stems are much slimmer.

SPIRAEA x VANHOUTTEI
Spiraea

ZONES 4–5

Spiraeas are of many kinds, some, like this lovely white-flowered garden hybrid, which arose in Belgium over a hundred years ago from two oriental parents and flowers in spring, to others of quite different habit which bloom pink in summer and originated in North America. All in their individual way make a valuable contribution to the garden display.

S. x vanhouttei forms clusters of white flowers along its arching branches, which can be up to 5ft (1.6m) long, and is generally propagated from hardwood cuttings inserted in gritty soil in a frame in late autumn. Softwood cuttings can also be used in early or midsummer, again in a frame or greenhouse.

S. x bumalda 'Anthony Waterer' flowers pink in mid to late summer and is a shorter, more compact shrub, suitable for the front rank of a graded display. Apart from cuttings, as mentioned above, its growth is such that a large thriving plant can be divided to give several rooted pieces.

S. menziesii is typical of the tall American species with spikes rather than flat clusters of pink flowers. It is of suckering habit – and can become a nuisance in some places – so it can also quite easily be propagated by removing a few of these suckers that have made sufficient roots to survive alone.

TAXUS BACCATA
Yew

ZONE 6

Yew is a most valuable and versatile garden plant, since, though plain in appearance, it is used for hedges, which clip satisfactorily to give a smooth and architectural finish – usually with only one clipping per year as against several for privet *(Ligustrum ovalifolium)*. Yew is also valued for topiary work, as it is a moderately quick grower which can be trained and clipped into a great variety of shapes – either formal and geometric or to represent birds and animals, such as the favourite, peacock.

Yew is most easily and cheaply reproduced from its seeds, which it bears in the red fruits known as arils. These must be stratified for six months before they are sown in spring, to break their dormancy. Spread the harvested fruits between layers of sharp sand in a pot or tin box, which is aerated, yet protected from hungry vermin, and stand it at the base of a cold north wall during the winter. Clean the seeds from any remaining flesh in the spring and sow. It will take perhaps four years to obtain good-sized plants 2–2½ft (60–75cm) high, so it demands patience.

Alternatively, semi-hardwood cuttings made from side shoots can be rooted in late summer or autumn in a frame or greenhouse. Remove the lower leaves and dip in rooting hormone before inserting in a sand/peat rooting mix.

Choice yews, such as the golden-leaved varieties are usually raised by grafting on to *Taxus baccata* rootstocks.

VIBURNUM TINUS
Laurustinus

ZONES 7–8

This glossy leaved evergreen with neat foliage and clusters of white flowers opening in succession from pink buds in mild spells throughout the winter is widely planted in gardens, as a single shrub, or in groups to form an informal screen. It is strongly hardy and tolerates seaside conditions too. 'Eve Price' is a choice form with pink-tinged blooms. A pleasing variegated form that flowers in early spring is sometimes marketed, which is a favourite of mine, but it is liable to damage in cold exposed districts.

Such a useful shrub is more likely than most to need propagating cheaply and easily. Luckily this is possible from semi-hardwood cuttings in a frame between midsummer and early autumn, from hardwood cuttings in a frame in late autumn or early winter, or by layering suitable low-growing branches between mid spring and late summer. Sufficient success should be possible with such a choice of methods to produce all the plants needed, given a mature stock plant to start with.

WEIGELA FLORIDA 'VARIEGATA'

ZONE 5

This lovely flowering shrub from Northern China is deciduous, so is only decorative from spring to autumn, but it can make a most valuable contribution to the garden picture. Its pleasant clusters of pink flowers, somewhat reminiscent of honeysuckle, to which it is distantly related, open in late spring and early summer on 6–7ft (2m) high bushes. The leaves of the 'Variegata' form have cream edges and green centres

A number of named varieties of the species, with plain green leaves, are offered, including rich red 'Eva Rathke', 'Mont Blanc' with white blooms and 'Esperance' a pale rose. Other forms include 'Foliis Purpureis' with purple foliage and 'Looymansii Aurea' with pale gold leaves.

All these weigelas are easily propagated from semi-hardwood cuttings during the summer or from hardwood cuttings taken in early winter, using a frame to protect them while they root. Remove side shoots with a heel of older growth, trim, dip in a rooting hormone, then root in a sandy mixture.

Trees

ACER PALMATUM
Japanese Maple

ZONE 5

T he acers or maples are a large genus, which includes small dainty Japanese trees and robust American species several times their size.

Acer species germinate quite well from seeds – the fat part of those 'keys' (samaras) that we see twirling to the ground in autumn. But the many special choice forms can only be perpetuated vegetatively and this is usually done by grafting a stem from the desirable form on to a vigorous rootstock of a related species that is not in itself particularly decorative. But grafting is not a job for the beginner, though

I would encourage you to experiment with this technique once you feel confident about those dealt with in this book.

We are left, then, with seed sowing. Collect seeds from suitable small trees in the autumn when they seem to be ripe but before they can become mouldy or be eaten by animals or just lost in the undergrowth after they have fallen. Dry them off and store cool until spring, when they can be sown in pots of gritty compost. Seeds of choice Japanese maples will not be certain to reproduce their parents' characteristics exactly, but you should get some interesting seedlings and be able to tell at an early stage which are worth growing on. If, as an alternative, you sow bought seeds of a good strain, you should do even better.

CERCIS SILIQUASTRUM
Judas Tree

ZONE 6

The Judas tree, so called because legend has it that Judas Iscariot hanged himself upon one of these trees, is a delight when smothered in its rose-pink pea flowers in late spring. Its round somewhat fleshy dark green leaves are quite distinctive and pleasing too. A mature tree can bear heavy crops of purple-tinted seedpods from midsummer and these provide us with the means to raise more such trees.

Allow the seeds to ripen well before harvesting them. This may need a particularly hot summer. Sow the seeds in mid spring in a greenhouse at a temperature of 65°F (18°C) to get them off to a good start. Grow them on gradually in successively larger pots, but be warned that they grow slowly and it can take some years to produce even a small tree that will flower. Its foliage justifies a place for an immature tree, but once you have seen a Judas tree in flower you will not be satisfied until you have flowers on your own.

The North American Redbud, *Cercis canadensis,* is a related tree and much more widely grown in America than *C. siliquastrum.* It is cultivated similarly.

EUCALYPTUS GUNNII
Blue Gum, Cider Gum

ZONE 8

Eucalyptus are now so widely planted across the world in subtropical and even milder temperate areas that it is hard to take it in that they all originated from Australia. They thrive in Mediterranean countries and in California and *E. gunnii* is all too happy in quite a cool climate. A handsome tree, its one fault is that it grows very quickly and is therefore probably too tall for a small garden. Its most attractive feature is its juvenile foliage, which is a lovely pale silvery blue and roughly oval in shape. This is quite distinct from the adult foliage, which is dark green, long, elliptical and curved like a sickle.

Flower arrangers in particular love the juvenile foliage for use in vases and arrangements of all sorts. Where a focal point with this colouring is called for in a garden, a young tree can be planted and kept pollarded, so that it forms a succession of young shoots bearing only juvenile foliage.

To acquire one of these trees free, or almost so, buy a packet of seeds and sow them in a pot in a cool greenhouse in spring. It will be a year or two before you have the tree you have dreamt of, but eucalyptus are rapid growers.

Juvenile foliage

Adult foliage

Prop the wound open slightly with a little sphagnum moss, then wrap whole area with more moss.

Enclose damp moss in a transparent polythene sheet bandage. Seal at each end with tape to prevent drying out.

Completed air layer. Roots will become visible after 6–8 weeks if layer succeeds.

Wound stem selected for air layering by cutting obliquely half way through thickness of stem.

Dust the wound with hormone rooting powder.

MAGNOLIA x SOULANGIANA

ZONE 5

This lovely spring-flowering tree can be a picture, provided its purple-pink flushed white chalices escape browning by frost or searing cold wind. In many a garden it is the centrepiece of the spring display, among a host of bulbs and wallflowers. There are various special forms of it, too, such as rose-purple 'Lennei' and pure white 'Alba Superba'.

These trees can be propagated by orthodox layering – burying a low-growing shoot in the ground after wounding it near a leaf joint, so that it roots to form a new plant, which can then be severed from the parent and planted elsewhere or by air layering. This is a means of layering or rooting a shoot that cannot be bent down to the ground.

Instead, a shoot is wounded in the same way, then the wound is propped open, treated with rooting hormone, surrounded with damp sphagnum moss and sealed in a clear plastic bandage. This is done between mid spring and late summer. After a few weeks roots start to appear within the bandage as the shoot forms roots. When these are sufficiently advanced, the shoot can be carefully detached and potted up to be grown on into a new young tree.

Softwood cuttings can be rooted in spring in a greenhouse in heat (70°F/21°C) and a close atmosphere in a propagating case.

Magnolia species (but not any of the hybrids or choice selections) can be raised from seeds sown in spring or autumn in a frame or greenhouse.

RHUS TYPHINA
Stag's Horn Sumach

ZONE 3

This North American tree, from the eastern side of that continent, is valued most perhaps for its brilliant autumn leaf tints of scarlet and gold, but its feathery compound leaves are also valued for their shape and texture. This is extra delightful in the form known as 'Laciniata', whose leaflets are themselves deeply toothed. Then there are the strange maroon red clusters of flowers, which you either like or hate.

This is generally a small tree, in cultivation reaching some 10ft (3m) although in its native eastern USA it grows much taller. It is quick to sucker if its roots are damaged by soil cultivation – even sometimes if they are not. This makes one the gift of new plants, which can be cut from their parents' roots and carefully lifted to plant elsewhere. There is another side to this, of course. It can develop suckers where you do not want them – in a lawn, among treasured decorative plants you do not wish to disturb. You then have to tolerate its behaviour or ban it from your garden altogether.

Besides using suckers in this way, you can produce youngsters from root cuttings, which is little more than taking the suckering phenomenon into the greenhouse or frame. Do this in mid winter and they will start to show vigorous signs of life in the spring.

———————

65

Rock Plants

A vigorous clump of the
'Atropurpurea' form.

Clump teased apart with the
hands to give two new plants.

Plants set out about 22.5cm (9in)
apart to carpet the area allotted
to this plant.

AJUGA REPTANS
Bugle

ZONES 2–3

This creeping, ground-covering plant is grown primarily for the ornamental foliage of its special forms, known as 'Variegata', 'Atropurpurea' and 'Burgundy Glow', though its 4in (10cm) high spikes of blue flowers in late spring are an added bonus. It is well enough behaved to plant in a rock garden, but is perhaps best used for ground cover. Here it is necessary to remove any weeds that creep in while it is becoming established.

Propagation, as you will have guessed, is simple – just lift and separate sections of the spreading carpet of growth and transplant them where required. This is best done in autumn or spring, but other times are possible provided conditions are not extreme. This is a good plant for producing material for a charity sale, as its rich purple, or cream and pale green, leaves are attractive, even a small specimen.

ANTENNARIA DIOICA
Cat's Foot,
Common Pussy-toes

ZONE 2

This little silvery-leaved rock plant is grown for the sake of its leaf colour, its white or rose-pink daisy flowers being quite insignificant. It spreads to form a decorative carpet of foliage which can create a pleasing contrast to other plants with green foliage and, of course, the bright colours of many other flowers.

Antennaria, which is native to Europe, including Scandinavia and the Arctic, and the Caucasus, roots as it spreads, so it is quite simple to remove rooted pieces from the rim of a clump and plant them separately to grow on. This is best done in spring in a frame or cool greenhouse. Where a lot are required, they can be set out like pricked-out seedlings in seed trays. They are sometimes used in this way to provide the silver colouring in floral clocks and carpet beds.

ARABIS FERDINANDII-COBURGII '*VARIEGATA*'

ZONE 7

While not as widespread and well known as the common rock cress, *A. albida (A. caucasica),* this is a particularly pleasing and trouble-free rock plant, which forms spreading clumps of cream-edged green leaves and generous clusters of starry white flowers in early spring. It roots as it spreads – a natural layerer, in fact – so this provides the obvious means of propagating it. This is best done in spring, preferably after flowering.

Seeds, sown in late spring or early summer, in a seedbed outdoors, offer the best means of raising many of the different forms of *Arabis caucasica,* of which there are white, pink and deep rose hues. The double white form has to be propagated vegetatively, by dividing up existing clumps in spring or by rooting half-ripe cuttings in a frame during the summer.

Besides making vigorous plants for masking and cascading over low walls and rock banks, arabis can be used in small clumps as a ground planting for formal beds of spring bulbs – white arabis with yellow narcissi or tulips, pink arabis with white narcissi or tulips, and many other artistic combinations.

AUBRIETA DELTOIDEA
Rock Cress

ZONE 4

This must be number one rock plant for the spring, as symbolic of that season as daffodils and tulips. A strong grower, easy to please, it will soon clothe a rock bank or low wall with cascades of flowers – not all lilac-mauve, but in pink and reddish shades too.

Harden your heart after it has flowered and give your plants a severe haircut, clipping them back to the basic clump of growth. They will soon make fresh growth which will flower well again the next spring and you will have avoided plants with bare centres.

Good strains of seed are available and can be sown in spring like other hardy bedding plants. They will make sturdy little plants by autumn that can be planted out then to flower the following spring.

The choicest colours, like purple 'Dr Mules', pink 'Dawn' and red 'Crimson Bedder' have to be perpetuated by dividing the clumps in autumn. Alternatively, you can take basal cuttings in a cold frame in late spring or early summer. Suitable cutting material is produced after the plants are cut back, following flowering. Prepare cuttings about 2in (5cm) long and insert them in moist, gritty rooting medium.

ERICA HERBACEA (ERICA CARNEA)
Winter-flowering Heather, Spring Heather

ZONE 5

Heathers in considerable variety, both of flower colour and leaf colour as well as season of display, are now sold by the tens of thousands. Apart from their beauty and variety, they make fine ground cover, keeping out all the weeds once they have completed blanketing the soil.

Erica herbacea varieties, like 'Springwood Pink' and 'Springwood White', 'King George' and 'Vivellii' are much valued for their cheerful colouring in winter and early spring. There are many other heathers to choose from to provide colour and interest right round the year. All are propagated similarly.

Easiest method is to remove rooted pieces from established plants. If you lift the stems around the edge of a clump, you could find some of them have made roots part way along their length and can be severed and transplanted to form new plants. This can be encouraged to happen artificially by mounding the centres of the plants with a sand/peat mixture into which the stems will root, so they can later be removed. This is best done in mid spring while growth is vigorous but the weather is not hot.

Stem cuttings provide the usual alternative. Take softwood stem cuttings about 1–1½in (2.5–3.5cm) long, between early summer and early autumn and insert them in trays of sandy/peaty mixture to root. Grow them on steadily until they are large enough to plant out. These cuttings will, of course, reproduce the characteristics of the parent plant exactly.

ERIGERON (MUCRONATUS) KARVINSKIANUS
Fleabane

ZONE 9

This charming little daisy from Mexico, only 8in (20cm) high but spreading 2ft (60cm), flowers profusely all summer long and is as true a rock plant as you could find, since it thrives in hot, dry crevices. It forms plenty of viable seeds, so it is generous with self-sown seedlings. In fact, one's practical problem may be in suppressing its bounding enthusiasm.

It specially loves to germinate and grow in the crevices in paving. An occasional plant left to break up a bare expanse of paving can be a bonus, but it is so irrepressible that it will need frequent curbing. Nonetheless, I find it a little treasure.

Propagation need consist of no more than transplanting its self-sown seedlings to the spots in which you want them. If you are just starting, however, a packet of seeds will soon provide you with more than enough plants. They are best sown in spring, so they have a long season of growth ahead of them.

ERINUS ALPINUS
Alpine Liverbalsam, Summer Starwort

ZONE 4

This tiny rock plant, 4in (10cm) tall when in bloom, is most generous with its flowers in late spring and early summer. It is literally a rock plant, revelling in the cracks and crannies in rocks or paved paths, in which it will self-sow quite prolifically. The individual plants, though perennial, are not long-lived, but they seed themselves quite generously enough to keep your stock going once you have started with them.

Their flowers may be lavender-pink, crimson-purple or white and named varieties are available in these colours – 'Albus' being white, 'Dr Hanelle' crimson and 'Mrs Charles Boyle' pink.

Erinus is raised from seeds, sown where you wish the plants to flower, in spring. They come reasonably true from seed if you sow a good strain. They prefer well drained soil that is not too rich – as you might expect when they thrive so happily in paving crevices.

POLYGONUM AFFINE
Himalayan Fleece-flower, Knotweed

ZONE 3

This spreading rock plant from the Himalayan region has several claims to our attention. Its mat of green foliage is neat and useful for carpeting bare ground to suppress weeds. In late summer it produces spikes of pink flowers, which show up well against the foliage. Then, as colder days arrive, their pink gradually turns to rusty red but remains decorative for many weeks. It is then altogether a specially decorative plant for late summer and autumn, and useful the remainder of the year.

Plants can be divided in the spring, for their prostrate growths tend to root as they go, offering an easy means of propagation. In addition, half-ripe cuttings can be taken from the plants in late summer and rooted in a frame, following the usual technique, including the use of rooting hormone.

SAXIFRAGA x URBIUM
London Pride

ZONE 7

London Pride is one of the most widely planted of the large saxifrage genus, though it is more likely to be used as a path edging or as ground cover than as a rock garden plant. It forms neat, quite large rosettes of fleshy leaves, which develop daughter rosettes around their bases to produce a gradually spreading carpet of growth – hence its value as ground cover. In late spring it produces tall stems of tiny blush-pink flowers of a generally dainty fairy-like appearance. It will grow in light shade but flowers best in sun.

Propagation is quite straightforward, by detaching rooted offsets – each a rosette and a short length of stem with some fibrous roots – which will establish readily in a suitable open gritty soil containing enough peat or other water-holding material. Plants are best divided in spring when they have most vigour and a long season of growth ahead of them.

Many other saxifrage species, such as the silver-leaved Snail Saxifrage *S. cochlearis,* can be propagated in a similar way, though their rosettes are much smaller and they may need somewhat closer attention to become established.

SEDUM SPATHULIFOLIUM
Stonecrop

ZONE 5

There are many species of sedum, succulent-leaved carpeting plants, the best of which are suitable for rock garden planting. *Sedum spathulifolium,* or its two popular forms, pale blue-green 'Cappa Blanca' and brownish mauve 'Purpureum', both with a whitish bloom on their leaves, are also beloved of those gardeners whose job it is to design and plant floral clocks and carpet beds showing coats of arms and suchlike.

These are easy plants, tolerant particularly of dry soil and full sun. Their rosettes of leaves each form tiny youngsters around themselves, which soon mature to do the same. Such rosettes whether already rooted or not, can be detached and inserted in moist sandy mixture in spring without artificial heat to form independent plants. One need never be without plants, for they multiply readily.

It is possible to raise these plants from seed too, but if they are offered as part of a mixture of sedum species they may be outnumbered by other perhaps less decorative kinds.

SEMPERVIVUM
Houseleek

ZONE 4

The common houseleek was once grown on the roofs of country cottages, hence its scientific name *S. tectorum,* but sempervivums have come a long way since then, with many choice varieties collected from the mountains of Europe. It is now possible to make a hobby of growing a collection of these plants alone, with rosettes of various shades of green and purple, some with purple or red tips to the leaves that form their rosettes.

Propagation is simple enough. As rosettes reach maturity, they naturally form tiny daughter rosettes around themselves, which in turn grow and multiply, so that if left alone they form spreading colonies inspiring their familiar name of hen-and-chickens. But these offsets, each with a short stem and few roots, can be detached and planted in a gritty medium to form new plants. In fact, they are so keen to multiply that rosettes that have not yet formed any roots can safely be detached and inserted in similar soil mixture, where they will soon make themselves at home and root.

In this way, it is quite simple to multiply those varieties one has and exchange surplus rosettes with other collectors for new forms. Or you may just prefer to admire an expanding collection! This simple propagation can be undertaken at almost any time that the temperature is above 45°F (7°C) and not scorching hot.

THYMUS SERPYLLUM
Thyme

ZONE 3

Ornamental thymes can make a striking contribution to the garden scene in early summer, when they are in full bloom and enthusiastically worked by bees and butterflies. For the rest of the year they merge into the background, forming modest carpets of green foliage.

They can be planted in suitable rock garden pockets, but the most attractive arrangement is to plant a 'lawn' of thyme, perhaps in several colours, to form an eye-catching display at flowering time. A variation upon this idea is an 'alpine lawn', carpeted with thyme, decorated with a few small rocks and dwarf conifers and given interest at other times by clusters of miniature bulbs thrusting up through the thyme – crocuses, winter aconites, snowdrops, *Iris reticulata* and many more.

Propagation is quite simple – yes, by dividing up the clumps, as this little creeper makes roots as it spreads over the soil, so it is easy to lift pieces to start fresh colonies elsewhere.

You can raise thyme from seeds, but division gives results so much quicker that it is rarely worth considering – provided you have a plant to divide, of course!

Bedding/Display Plants

CHEIRANTHUS CHEIRI
Annual Wallflower

Wallflowers are favourite cottage garden flowers, valued for the contribution they make to the main display of spring colour in the garden, particularly in public gardens where they form a groundwork to displays of tulips. Their scent is glorious too.

All are, of course, hybrids, so though you could sow home-saved seeds, you would be far wiser to use those from a reputable seedsman, which have been carefully selected and should be true to name. Then you can expect to have the colours and sizes of plant that you want – vital where they are to be companions to other plants or bulbs and any mistakes will scream out!

Sow seeds outdoors in a seedbed in late spring or early summer. Keep moist and dust against flea beetle if necessary. (This pest bites tiny holes in their leaves.) Transplant to nursery rows in mid summer to grow on, then to their flowering positions in mid autumn. Though plants can well survive the winter, you will find their blooms deteriorate. Many will go streaky, which is a sign of virus disease. They should be burnt to stop the trouble spreading.

ANTIRRHINUM HYBRIDS
Snapdragon

Antirrhinums in a remarkable range of colours, some soft, some brilliant, varying in height from 8in (20cm) dwarfs to 30in (75cm) giants and with flowers of several different shapes, can provide many weeks of colour in the summer garden. They may form blocks of contrasting colours or form a groundwork punctuated by tall 'dot' plants and edged by some distinctive dwarf kind of plant. They be used as decorative tub or windowbox flowers.

All this is possible from a few modestly priced packets of seed, sown in a cool greenhouse (55°F/13°C) in late winter to yield plants ready for planting in the garden in late spring.

Though by nature perennial, antirrhinums are always grown as annuals, so the plants are discarded at the end of their season of glory.

Leaving spent flower spikes on one's own plants to set and ripen seeds is not advisable, however. It is not only discouraging the production of more flowers and thus spoils the display, but being hybrid seeds, the resultant seedlings will not come true to type and their flowers are likely to be disappointing.

ARGYRANTHEMUM FRUTESCENS
(CHRYSANTHEMUM FRUTESCENS)
Marguerite

ZONE 10

This shrubby relative of *Chrysanthemum* is often seen in formal summer displays, perhaps in an urn, and, though simple, its pure white blooms are most attractive, especially when contrasted with scarlet geraniums. A native perennial of the Canary Islands, this old favourite plays a valuable role in the garden. Plants are often housed in a frost-free greenhouse or conservatory for the winter and brought out for the summer season. Year by year they form ever larger woody stemmed specimens.

To make more of these plants, or replace them if they become too old and large, you can take stem cuttings. In spring, softwood cuttings will enable you to start fresh plants, in summer half-ripe cuttings provide further opportunities.

If you yearn for something a little more special, then how about the yellow-flowered 'Jamaica Primrose'? There are also pink-flowered marguerites too, so there is no need for monotony.

DAHLIA

A dahlia, lifted after one season's growth from a cutting, showing its plump tubers. Plants with several stems can be cut into several pieces, each with at least one stem, several tubers and strong growth buds where stems and tubers join to form new plants.

Dahlias come in a dazzling variety of sizes, colours and flower shapes and are useful for several distinct purposes – for creating magnificently coloured borders in high summer, for producing armfuls of lovely cut flowers for vases indoors, the smaller one for tub and patio decoration, many of the choicest for winning prizes at shows. But there are just a few ways of propagating them, common to them all – though preferences vary somewhat according to the type of dahlia.

As dahlias are highly bred hybrids, the choicest named varieties are all raised from cuttings or by dividing the tubers of existing plants, so they reproduce their parents' characteristics faithfully. Some good seed strains are available and quite adequate for bedding dahlias, like 'Coltness Gem', those compact bushy 1½ft (45cm) high plants used with the geraniums and petunias for bright summer colour. Sow them with the other bedding plant seeds in late winter in warmth (55–60°F/13–15°C) and prick them out into small pots when well rooted.

Cuttings and divisions are both produced in spring, but depend equally upon tubers that have been carefully lifted, dried off and overwintered until late winter, when they are coaxed into life with some warmth (55°F/13°C) and moisture. These produce young shoots, which can be taken as basal cuttings while they are short (about 2–3in/5–7.5cm) and sturdy and certainly before they become hollow. (All mature dahlia stems are hollow.) Cut them off close to the tuber. (Some gardeners prefer to take a little of the mature tissue with them.)

Dip all the cuttings in a dilute insecticide solution if there is any risk of aphid infestation, then in rooting hormone (liquid or powder). Then insert them in pots of gritty rooting mixture – e.g. equal parts peat and sand, or peat and perlite. Keep them in a warm humid place to root. When their perkiness shows that they have made roots, gradually accustom them to more normal temperatures, then pot them individually and grow them on until eventually they are large enough (and the weather is mild enough) to plant out.

Tubers overwintered from the previous season can, of course, be planted out without being divided. Time this so that their new young shoots do not appear above ground until all serious risk of frost is past – usually in mid to late spring to appear in early summer.

Where extra plants are wanted, the clusters of tubers can be carefully divided with a knife, making sure that each new portion has at least one tuber, a strong healthy crown bud (at the base of the stem where it joins the tuber) and some healthy fibrous roots. These can be planted out at the same time as the complete plants, but it is an advantage to divide them earlier and get them well started in a greenhouse if you have the space and warmth (about 55°F/13°C).

As dahlias are subject to virus diseases and the tubers can rot in winter, do inspect them closely before propagating and discard anything doubtful. Also rogue out and destroy any with abnormal (mottled, crinkled or stunted) foliage when they leaf out.

DIGITALIS PURPUREA
Foxglove

ZONE 4

This familiar flower, 3–5ft (90–150cm) tall, is a biennial, which forms a ground-hugging rosette of leaves in its first year from seed and a tall flower stem in its second, after which it dies. By nature a woodland plant, it is best grown in informal groups in a woodland garden or in moist soil near water. Its novel use as a display plant with hyacinths and other hardy flowers in a cool airy conservatory at the Longwood Gardens near Philadelphia could be worth imitating.

The wild species with bells hanging from only one side of the spike comes readily from seeds, which can be sown outdoors in a seed bed in late spring or early summer and pricked out in nursery rows when large enough. Plant in flowering positions in mid autumn to flower the next spring.

The choicer Excelsior Hybrids in mixed colours with flowers right round the spike which have largely superseded the species in gardens, are also easy from bought seeds, but seeds saved from one's own plants are likely to revert to a poorer standard and give more modest flowers.

As a biennial, the foxglove cannot, of course, be divided.

PELARGONIUM ZONALE
Geranium

ZONE 10

Geraniums are perennial sub-shrubs and form the mainstay of so many summer bedding displays – not only in beds and borders, but in windowboxes, tubs, urns and hanging baskets. Their bright colours and their reliability have together contributed to their popularity.

The ease with which they can be propagated must also have played its part in gaining them favour, for they are easy to root from half-ripe cuttings in late summer and early autumn. Just take suitable side shoots of the current year's growth about 3–4in (7.5–10cm) long, trim them across immediately beneath a leaf joint, remove all the lower leaves and the tiny leaf-like stipules, which could wither and provide entry for fungus disease, then dip in hormone rooting preparation and insert in a moist gritty mixture. Kept moist but not too wet and shaded from fierce sun, they should root without trouble within 3–4 weeks.

Such cuttings will also root readily in water, though the roots they make will then be softer and more liable to be damaged when they are potted up. So it pays to pot them first into a soft, largely peat-based mixture, to allow them to toughen up. After this treat them like any other geranium cuttings.

As geraniums are very amenable, it is worth trying to root cuttings out of the most favoured period, or to root shorter pieces – even just one bud and leaf – if it is urgent to obtain plants at such a time.

A considerable selection of F1 hybrid seeds is now offered, making it possible to raise geraniums in many colours just a few months before flowering them. But they need quite a long season of growth, so they must be sown in mid winter if they are to start flowering before midsummer. If sown later with the bulk of the bedding plants, it could be late summer before you see any blooms. Sow in a temperature of 65–70°F (18–21°C) and keep them growing steadily by potting on or feeding as necessary to get strong bushy plants. If you wish, you can eventually root cuttings from these plants to overwinter them, though you may prefer to raise a fresh batch from seeds the following mid winter.

Ivy-leaved geraniums (*Pelargonium peltatum* hybrids) can also be propagated from half-ripe cuttings in late summer, though having thinner stems they are not quite so easy to root. A few seed strains are now available, but cuttings remain the chief method for these plants.

A well-developed plant could yield several cuttings. Yours may be part of an outdoor display, so do not cut it too hard.

Prepared half-ripe cutting about 10cm (4in) long. Lower leaves and stipules have been stripped off and base cut across just under a leaf joint.

Dip in hormone rooting preparation then insert round rim of pot of gritty compost.

TAGETES HYBRIDS
French and African Marigolds

A scintillating galaxy of French and African marigolds – which all originated in Mexico! – and hybrids between the two distinct races, is offered by seedsmen. Their sunny yellow and orange and rich mahogany-red blooms, their colours combined in a bewildering variety of ways in single and double flowers of many shapes and sizes, give a special vibrance to the summer display.

Tagetes of all kinds are, however, among the easiest of summer annuals to raise from seeds. Sow them in a cool greenhouse 50–55°F (10–13°C) in early spring and you will soon have many sturdy seedlings lined out in boxes eagerly growing towards planting day. But restrain your eagerness to put them out as a sneaky late frost can do them irreparable harm. Wait until such risks are past or at least minimal.

As with all hybrid flowers, you are advised not to try raising new plants from any ripe seeds they may produce, since these will not come true to type and are likely to be disappointing.

PETUNIA HYBRIDS

T he popularity of petunias has grown enormously since the seedsmen bred more weather resistance into their somewhat fragile blooms, developed more compact plants and added whole new ranges of colours and patterns to them, like the star-marked varieties and those veined a darker hue, plus picotees and glorious doubles too. There are plenty of petunias for that splash of summer colour, but also distinctive kinds for tubs and baskets and for use as pot plants. All are generous with their blooms, producing a long succession for many weeks.

Like other summer annuals, petunias are no trouble to raise from seeds. Sow them in late winter or early spring in a cool greenhouse and keep them growing steadily, ready for planting day in late spring, when frosts are over. Don't try saving seeds from your plants, as these are hybrids and will not come true to colour and form.

Climbers

BOUGAINVILLEA GLABRA

ZONE 10

This showy climber, or more correctly scrambler, since it does not twine or have adventitious roots like ivy, is only suitable for cultivation in the open in the most favoured climates, like that of California. But it is an easy conservatory plant in cooler areas, provided it can be kept frost free in winter. Its 'flowers' are in fact bracts, which is why they last so long. Each protects a cluster of three tiny white flowers which are rather insignificant in themselves. The most widely grown form has magenta purple bracts, but there are also orange and scarlet forms, which can together make quite a dazzling display on a fence or house or through a tree in a warm climate.

Bougainvilleas are often sold as flowering pot plants in temperate countries, with their stems wound round a wire hoop. Lovely though they are, this can give quite a false impression, for this plant is vigorous, not unlike a so-called climbing rose. So, if you want to save your potted bougainvillea and get the most from it, you need to release its stems and train them up canes or on a tall narrow trellis and repot it in a large pot or tub of nourishing compost. If satisfied, it will make a plant 6–10ft (2–3m) tall.

To produce extra plants from your original, take semi-hardwood cuttings in mid to late summer, rooting them in pots of gritty mixture in heat in a greenhouse.

Remove a semi-ripe shoot about 15cm (6in) long.

Strip off lower leaves.

Cut across just under a leaf joint to leave 10cm (4in) long.

CLEMATIS SPECIES & HYBRIDS

ZONES 3 – 6

A wide variety of clematis, ranging from large-flowered hybrids like 'Nelly Moser' and 'Jackmanii' to species smothered in much smaller flowers like *Clematis tangutica, C. recta, C. montana* and *C. macropetala,* are now planted to cover house walls, trellis, fences and old tree stumps and to clamber into shrubs and trees.

One of a kind in a garden could well be sufficient, but you might wish to produce some plants to give as presents, or to root material from someone's plant. So how is this done?

There are, in fact, several methods. Most favoured is to prepare leaf bud cuttings from the soft spring growth. These should be about 1in (2.5cm) long and cut just above a leaf and its attendant bud but some way beneath it. Leave only one leaf. Insert in a gritty medium in a warm humid atmosphere to root between mid spring and early summer. This could be a propagator in a greenhouse or a polythene-covered pot on a warm windowsill. Ventilate occasionally to avoid stagnant air and the risk of fungus disease. Once the cuttings have rooted, gradually harden them off and then pot separately to grow into strong young plants.

An alternative method is to layer low-growing shoots that can be brought down to soil level, wounded near a leaf joint and treated with rooting hormone, then buried in some gritty soil mixture, such as old soil-based potting mixture, to root. Clematis can be layered between mid spring and late summer. Peg the layers into the soil so they cannot be disturbed while they are rooting, and stake their tips with canes so they form shapely young plants. Let them root well before severing from the parent plant and lifting and transplanting elsewhere. Those layered early may be ready by autumn, but it is generally wiser to wait until the following spring before moving them, as they then have more vigour and do not have to face a winter just afterwards.

Many of the clematis species can be grown from seeds, which are best sown outdoors in early to mid spring. Leave seedlings to root well before transplanting to make strong plants ready for planting in their flowering positions. Such patience pays off. If you act prematurely you could lose them.

Mature young shoot of variegated ivy suitable for making cuttings.

Strip off all lower leaves.

Shorter pieces of stem can be used as leaf bud cuttings.

HEDERA HELIX
English Ivy

ZONE 5

Ivies have become widely popular in the last two or three decades, as their foliage is neat and often coloured or variegated and the plants are highly versatile – as pot plants, for clothing walls, cascading over walls and for ground cover. Take just 'Glacier' (pale green and cream variegations), 'Buttercup' (gold in full sun) and 'Goldheart' (deep green with butter-yellow centre) as examples of their many virtues.

We need to be able to propagate popular plants easily so the demand can be met promptly. Luckily, ivies are very obliging. Where their wandering stems touch the soil they will make roots, so it is then simple to lift and sever suitable rooted portions to make new plants. Rooting can be induced like this deliberately – and there is no need to wound the stems or use rooting hormone.

Stem cuttings, consisting of little more than one bud and leaf with a section of stem, will root if kept moderately warm and humid. This is a useful method for making many plants from a small amount of material. This is a job for midsummer in a greenhouse or frame, which are necessary to provide suitable close conditions.

Prepared leaf bud cutting, with lower leaves removed.

Cuttings inserted round edge of pot of gritty compost to root.

JASMINUM NUDIFLORUM
Winter Jasmine

ZONE 5

Although usually grown on a wall or fence, this jasmine is a scrambling plant whose propensity is to arch over and downwards – just right for the top of a bank or over the parapet of a wall. But it remains a splendid plant which is probably greatly undervalued because it is so tough and trouble free – besides being a valued winter flowerer. So take another look at it next time you see it!

Fortunately propagating it is equally easy and trouble-free. Where its drooping stems reach the soil, they will often form roots and can be severed and planted out when they are sufficiently developed to fend for themselves. They can as easily be layered like this deliberately – and there is no need to wound the stems or use rooting hormone. This can be done outdoors from mid-spring to late summer. If you want more plants, you could try serpentine layering, burying parts of a long stem with the intermediate parts left exposed, so you get several rooted pieces from each.

Hardwood cuttings can be inserted in slits in the soil, with sharp sand at the base in a frame in autumn and should be rooted by spring.

LONICERA PERICLYMENUM
'BELGICA'
Honeysuckle, Woodbine

ZONE 4

What could be more delightful than a sweet-smelling honeysuckle trained over a front porch, near an open window or over an arch or pergola? This, the so-called Early Dutch honeysuckle, is both colourful and fragrant and in bloom for a couple of weeks or so each season. Its colouring is a mixture of deep purplish pink and cream and is most attractive.

Where it is possible to bring a shoot or two down to the soil, this plant (and other kinds of honeysuckle) can be layered in the normal way between mid spring and later summer. Wound the shoot near a leaf joint, treat with rooting hormone, then bury and peg down in a gritty soil mixture to root. When adequately rooted – and do not hurry to move newly propagated plants – they can be severed from their parent, lifted and transplanted to develop into strong plants. Support them with canes to keep the new growth shapely.

Trained honeysuckles will probably not offer any suitable shoots for layering and so you will then need to turn to semi-hardwood cuttings to provide new plants. Root these in early to midsummer in a greenhouse or in mid-autumn in a frame. Again, allow them to root strongly before you attempt to lift and move them – preferably autumn for the early batch and spring for the later batch.

Most of the honeysuckles grown for garden decoration are hybrids, but any species you wish to grow, like yellow-flowered *Lonicera tragophylla* (Zone 6), can be raised from seeds sown in warmth in a greenhouse in spring.

PASSIFLORA CAERULEA
Passion Flower

ZONE 7

This Passion Flower needs a mild climate to flourish outdoors but is hardy enough to be grown outdoors in Britain, particularly on a warm wall in the milder parts of the country. In more favourable climates such as in California it should be possible to grow several other species as well and even enjoy their edible fruits.

The blue passion flower is grown for its fascinating and complex flowers, in which their early discoverers in Brazil decided they could see the various instruments used in Christ's passion, hence the plant's name.

To make more plants from existing stock, you can layer suitable low-growing shoots at any time between mid spring and late summer. Wound them near a leaf joint, dust this area with a rooting hormone preparation, then peg down in the soil – or preferably old soil-based potting mix – to root. Stake up the tip of the shoot, which will form the new plant, with a bamboo cane and peg the layer into the soil to keep it steady, so that any new roots are not damaged.

As an alternative, *Passiflora* can be rooted from leaf bud cuttings in a greenhouse in late spring or early summer. Take ½–1in (1.3–2.5cm) lengths of young growth, each with one leaf and its attendant bud, cut just above the bud and some way beneath it and insert in sand/peat mixture after dipping in rooting compound. Root in warm (65–70°F/ 18–21°C) humid conditions.

———————

SOLANUM CRISPUM
Potato Vine

ZONE 8

The blue potato vine, *S. crispum*, is a colourful shrubby scrambler of reasonably restrained growth which provides colour in mid to late summer – ideal for a length of rustic work or for covering a shed or summer house, perhaps. Its purple-blue flowers, identical in shape to those of the potato and tomato, each carry a distinctive bright yellow centre of stamens. 'Glasnevin' is a selected form often planted for its longer flowering season.

Fortunately this attractive plant is not difficult to raise from semi-hardwood cuttings of current season's shoots in mid to late summer in a greenhouse, where they can be dipped in a rooting hormone, inserted in a gritty mixture and kept warm and humid until they have rooted. After this, they can be potted individually in small pots, grown on and gradually hardened off, ready for their eventual move to the great outdoors.

———————

84

VITIS COIGNETIAE
Glory-vine

ZONE 5

This very strong growing vine from China and Japan can look magnificent both in green leaf in summer and when displaying its vivid red and purple tints in autumn, but it is essential to choose the site carefully where it can be given free rein, for its huge leaves can be 10in (25cm) or more across and its vigorous stems may wander well over 20ft (6m) in a season.

This desirable ornamental is propagated in the same way as its cousin, the grapevine (see next page).

VITIS VINIFERA
Grapevine

ZONE 6

Grapevines can be cultivated seriously and successfully in milder regions to yield wine grapes and if thinned, dessert fruits. But they can also be grown as purely ornamental wall and fence coverers, since their foliage is neat and pleasant and their bunches of tiny fruits quite decorative even when not brought to harvesting standard. The purple-leaved form 'Purpurea' and the hybrid 'Brant' are both specially decorative. In more favoured climates, like California and the Southern states of the USA, vines are widely planted over pergolas and other supports to provide shade from the hot sun.

However used, vines can be propagated with little difficulty from bud cuttings known also as eye cuttings or by layering. The cuttings are inserted in early mid winter in heat (70°F/ 21°C) in a propagator which provides them with a close atmosphere. Prepare cuttings from 1½in (3.5cm) lengths of one-year-old wood with a dormant bud at the top or in the centre. Those with the bud at the top are inserted upright in gritty rooting medium, the others are laid or pinned horizontally to the surface of a similar medium. Remove any other buds from the cuttings and cut away a sliver of bark from the underside of the horizontal cuttings and treat with hormone rooting powder to encourage rooting. Be sure that the cuttings are well rooted before moving and potting them individually.

Layering, during late spring and throughout summer, is done as for shrubs by just wounding a long shoot that can be bent down to the soil at a joint where you want it to root. Keep the wound – usually an oblique cut about 2in (5cm) long into the stem – open with a sliver of wood and bury it in a sand/peat soil mixture to make rooting more certain, keeping it moist during dry weather. Layers can be severed from the parent plant, lifted and planted elsewhere once they are well rooted.

Where several plants are wanted and the shoot is long enough, you can use the technique of serpentine layering, in which alternate sections of the stem are buried or left exposed to give a number of rooted layers, which can be treated just like single layers.

Select a length of mature but not too woody stem from a strong-growing vine

Cut stem across half way between each pair of buds.

Remove a sliver of bark from the side opposite the bud to expose the cambium layer, which will form roots.

Dust the wounded surface with hormone rooting powder.

Completed bud cutting or vine eye.

Press cutting horizontally into surface of rooting compost and await signs of growth.

PLUMBAGO CAPENSIS
Cape Leadwort, Cape Plumbago

ZONE 9

This lax-growing South African shrub is generally grown trained to a wall, though it does not in fact possess any natural means of clinging or scrambling. Fine for a garden with a Mediterranean climate, as in California, it demands the protection of a conservatory in more rigorous climates such as Britain, though a modest 45°F (7°C) will be enough to keep it safe through the cold season. It is smothered in ethereal blue flowers for months during summer – and there is a white form too.

However you intend to grow it, whether as plants grown as standards in large pots which are stood outdoors for summer decoration or plunged as 'dot plants' in formal bedding – plumbago can be rooted from soft or semi-hardwood cuttings in pots of gritty medium in a greenhouse between late spring and midsummer. Dip in rooting hormone, give them about 70°F (21°C) and keep them in a close atmosphere until well rooted. Then pot individually in small pots, grow on in larger and larger pots and accustom to cooler temperatures. Once you have enjoyed this plant's delightful flowers, you will not want to be without it.

WISTERIA SINENSIS
Chinese Wisteria

ZONE 5

Surely one of the most breathtaking sights of late spring must be the cascade of pale lilac blossom of a mature wisteria, perhaps trained across the front of a red brick house, or over a large pergola. It is arguably the most ornamental of all flowering twiners. The individual skeins of pea flowers can range from 8in–1ft (20–30cm) long and there are white and dark purple forms too. They can be at least twice as long as this in the 'Macrobotrys' form of the Japanese *W. floribunda*.

Such magnificence stems from a particularly vigorous plant, which has to be pruned twice a year to keep it within bounds, once it is well established. But its long growths, left unpruned for the purpose, offer us a means of making new plants. Those near enough to the ground can be bent down, wounded near a leaf joint and pegged into a peat/sand mixture to form layers. When well rooted these can be severed from the parent and transplanted or potted up. It is sometimes possible to try serpentine layering, burying several parts of a shoot to give a number of new plants. Layer shoots from mid spring to late summer and leave them undisturbed until the following season.

It is also possible to root hardwood cuttings of wisteria in a greenhouse in early winter.

Bulbs

ALLIUM CAERULEUM
Blue Globe Onion,
Ornamental Onion

ZONES 2-3

The ornamental onions are often shunned because of their oniony scent, which you may consider out of place in the flower garden. However, the many species between them offer blue, white, red, pink, purple and yellow (10 in/20 cm) and A. christophii (silver lilac) (2ft/60cm). so prolific where they are well pleased as to become a nuisance. There is no problem with propagation, since the clus-ters of bulbs multiply quickly and the blooms set seeds and provide self-sown seedlings.

Among the most attractive to look at are *A. caeruleum* (blue) (2ft/60cm), *A. ostrowskianum* (rose-pink) (6in/15cm), *A. neapolitanum* (white) (2ft/60cm), *Allium moly* (yellow) (10in/20cm) and *.A christophii* (silver lilac) (2ft/60cm).

To get started with alliums, you could buy a few bulbs to plant in autumn, or sow seeds in late winter outdoors, for most are bone hardy. Despite their reputation for smelling unpleasant, the blooms can be cut and displayed in vases indoors without discomfort.

CROCUS TOMASINIANUS

ZONE 5

Crocuses are particularly welcome flowers, since they appear without fail early in the year while spring is still struggling to reveal its full beauty to us in the face of often chill winds and the possibility of snow. All the more welcome then are crocuses whose clusters of corms do not merely hold their own from year to year but actually multiply. These very clearly offer us 'plants for free'. All we need do is lift and divide the clumps every two or three years soon after they have flowered and replant them to form new colonies.

Crocus tomasinianus, an early flowerer, most impressive in its richer-coloured 'Whitewell Purple' and 'Taplow Ruby' forms, is a notably prolific multiplier. The widely planted larger-flowered purple and orange-yellow Dutch hybrids that bloom a week or two later are also good survivors and multiply, if not so prolifically. So make the best of all these to start fresh colonies in many parts of your garden. Then spring will be a far more exciting time as their blooms open wide in the warming sun to reveal brightly contrasting stigmata which add to the effect.

GALANTHUS NIVALIS
Snowdrop

ZONE 3

The snowdrop is one of our best-loved flowers mainly because it comes before almost all the other flowers in the annual pageant. It is a dainty beauty, yet perhaps we should take less notice of it if it flowered two months later. As it is, we rejoice to see new signs of life after the worst of the winter weather, so we should welcome a larger colony of them.

Here the basic need is to get them to flourish, then divide the clumps and replant. This should be done as soon as they have flowered – what is called planting them 'in the green' before their foliage can die down. They are then most likely to become re-established. This is a bulb that does not thrive on being dried off in the way daffodils and tulips are.

And how to get them to thrive? Primarily to treat them as woodland bulbs, giving them a good, deep, moist, cool, humus soil, so that they do not shrivel and die during the hot summer weeks. A scattering of bonemeal will not come amiss either.

LILIUM SPECIES & HYBRIDS

Many plants, some of them not even bulbs, are familiarly known as lilies, but it is only the many members of the genus *Lilium* that are true lilies. They include many breathtakingly beautiful flowers and, once you have learned to provide them with the kind of conditions they enjoy – deep, cool, moist peaty or leafy soil, sun for their heads, shade for their feet and protection from rough winds – you will want to grow ever more of them.

Many of them, fortunately, are now reasonably priced, though by no means cheap, and they are easier to grow than formerly, particularly since the development of the modern hybrids with their greater vigour and disease resistance. Unless money is no object, you will want to buy a couple of bulbs each of many varieties to try them out – and then, if possible, make more of them.

Well, fortunately this is possible. Each lily bulb is formed of a number of loose fleshy scales, which must, by the way, never be allowed to dry out in the way that daffodil and tulip bulbs are quite normally treated. Each of these scales, if detached from the bulb, will form a new bulb at its base if plunged into a moist mixture of peat and sand in a clear plastic bag (ventilated with a few holes so that they don't become stagnant and rot). Bags of scales can be hung on a line in a cool greenhouse until roots start to show through the bag. They can then be potted individually in small pots of similar medium and grown on gradually to maturity. This method of making more lilies is suitable for almost all, but there are other methods, of value for particular kinds.

If you have ever grown or had a close acquaintance with the orange-red lily 'Enchantment' or with the species *Lilium tigrinum,* the Tiger Lily (Zone 3), you may have been surprised or intrigued to find little 'bulbs' forming in the leaf axils on its stems. These bulbils, as they are correctly called, can be removed when ready (but before they fall and are lost) and 'sown' in trays of peat/sand mixture to grow into true bulbs. Only a few lilies behave in this way, but stem bulbils are most useful for making more of them.

Some lilies, of which *Lilium regale* (Zone 3), the Regal Lily, is outstanding, regularly form pods of viable seeds. These can be sown when ripe and will develop into strong young plants. *L. regale* will sometimes flower within two years of sowing seeds, though three years is more certain. As with other plants, only sow the seeds of lily *species,* since seeds of hybrids will not come true to type.

Growing lilies can become a fascinating hobby and lily propagating is an integral part of it.

Remove one or two scales from each bulb.

Put scales in moist sand/peat mixture in a polythene bag and seal, apart from few air holes. Hang up in warm place. Each scale should form a tiny new bulb at the base.

Fruit Bushes and Herbs

Cut suitable shoots of well-ripened current year's growth for use as hardwood cuttings. Remove all lower leaves, but leave all buds so that new plant suckers to form a stool of growths to bear fruits later.

RIBES NIGRUM
Blackcurrant

ZONE 4

Besides being a handsome fruit when its glossy black berries hang in generous clusters on the bushes in midsummer, and a tasty one when stewed and sweetened with sugar (or with dried fruit like dates, an interesting alternative), the blackcurrant is particularly valued for its high vitamin C content. So there is every reason to make a few extra plants and find some spot in the garden to grow them to cropping maturity. Note, though, that it is a hungry plant that responds to plenty of compost, manure and bonemeal, to replenish its energies and keep its roots cool and moist through the summer.

It is comparatively simple to strike hardwood cuttings of blackcurrant in the open ground in late autumn. Take cuttings 6–9in (15–23cm) long, cut them across just beneath a bud at the lower end and trim off the tip if the growth is soft. Be sure to leave all the buds intact on the cuttings, since blackcurrants are grown as 'stools', with new shoots springing from under the soil rather than from a short 'trunk' or clear stem.

Insert in a small slit trench with sharp sand trickled into the bottom, so that the cuttings are standing on this. Firm in well and leave nature to do the rest – apart from firming them in again every time frost lifts them.

The size of berries and the weight of crop will depend to a considerable extent on the named variety of currant you buy, so once you have found one you like, you will want to make more from it.

Remove small well-rooted pieces from side of clump to form new plants, or . . .

. . . tease clump apart to make several or even many new plants.

ALLIUM SCHOENOPRASUM
Chives

ZONES 2–3

This is a valuable culinary herb, easy to grow and at the same time quite acceptable as an ornamental plant, since its foliage is neat and its lavender or rose-coloured flowers in midsummer are quite attractive. So if you want a mild onion flavouring for salads or sandwiches and have little ground to spare, you could line out a few chive plants as a path edging in your flower garden.

Chives grow in much the same way as perennial border plants, forming expanding clumps of typical onion-like leaves and strong mats of fibrous roots. It is simple to break up these clumps during mild weather in the autumn or winter and plant out the smaller pieces to make plants for the next season.

They can also be raised from seeds sown in pots in spring, then planted out when large enough. This is a good way to start with chives, unless a friend cares to give you a small clump taken from his or her stock. Once you have chives well established, however, you cannot better division as the means for keeping a vigorous collection of plants going. (Don't be afraid, either, to cut back the foliage to near ground level if you want your plants to produce more tender foliage for eating.)

Set out new plants about 30cm (1ft) apart to grow into mature clumps.

RIBES GROSSULARIA
Gooseberry

ZONE 4

The gooseberry is a most useful and easily cultivated bush fruit for the home garden, and sometimes grown on a large scale. Provided it is grown in richly fertile soil and kept pruned, as it tends to make a jungle of growth if neglected, it is a reliable fruiter. But watch for its main enemies, the gooseberry sawfly, whose caterpillars can soon defoliate a bush in spring or early summer, and for birds pecking out the buds in late winter. Keep them away by criss-crossing the bushes with black cotton.

Bushes that become old can be replaced or new ones started quite easily from hardwood cuttings, taken in late autumn outdoors or in a frame. Remove the lower leaf buds from these cuttings so that the young plants you raise will grow on a clear stem or leg about 4in (10cm) long. If you do not do this, you will be be plagued by unwanted suckers. The cuttings should be about 8in (20cm) long, cut just beneath a leaf joint at the base and with any soft growth removed from the top. Retain only three or four leaf buds near the top to form the branches of the new bush you are creating.

RUBUS IDAEUS
Raspberry

ZONE 3

The raspberry is a naturally suckering plant, native to the temperate parts of Europe and Northern Asia. It is, of course, valued for its delicious fruits, ready to pick in mid summer and is widely grown for this purpose in gardens and commercially on a field scale for canning and preserving.

Many choice varieties have been developed over the years, outstanding for their flavour, the size of their fruits, the hardiness of the plants, or for some element of disease resistance. Once one has acquired canes of a variety one particularly likes, the question of how to make more plants, or renew the existing ones as they get older and bear less heavily, is bound to arise. The answer, of course, is to use those suckers.

Lift suitable vigorous healthy well rooted suckers and set them out in really fertile ground to form new rows of fruiting plants. But do note that proviso – that they are healthy – for raspberries are particularly vulnerable to virus diseases, transmitted from infected to healthy plants by migrating aphids. Any raspberries with blotchy pale coloured leaves that bear few if any fruits or show signs of stunting or distortion should be burned, not propagated from. If necessary, buy in fresh stock from nurserymen which is certified virus-free. But suckers remain a useful means of perpetuating healthy stock.

Index

Acknowledgements

The photographs of plant species on the following pages were supplied by Harry Smith Horticultural:
p5, 9, 10, 13, 18, 20, 22, 23, 24, 25 (both), 26 (both), 28 (both), 29, 30 (both), 31 (both), 32, 33 (both), 34 (both), 35, 36 (both), 37, 38, 39, 40 (both), 41, 42 (both), 43, 44, 45, 46 (both), 47 (both), 48 (three images), 49, 50, 52, 53 (both), 54 (both), 55, 56, 57 (three images), 58 (both), 59, 60, 61, 63 (both), 64, 65, 66, 67, 68, 69, 70, 71, 72, 73, 74, 75, 78, 80, 81 (both), 82, 83 (both), 84 (both), 85, 86, 87, 88, 91, 93 (both). The photograph of Erica flowers on p. 70 is supplied by Thompson and Morgan. All other plant species and all step by step photographs are © Quarto Publishing plc.

All jacket photos courtesy of Harry Smith Photographic Collection.